D1195996

SPIRIT, SAINTS AND IMMORTALITY

Many religions not only honour holy men and women, but believe that they are signs of the life to come. In Christianity this belief takes the form of the claim that the indwelling of the Holy Spirit, which sanctifies people and renews them in the likeness of God, is a 'first fruits' or 'earnest' of what is to come. This book considers the claim, mainly though not exclusively with reference to Christianity, and raises both philosophical and theological questions about it. It examines the ideas of the spirit of God, saintliness, likeness to God and immortality, and discusses the connections between them. It concludes that the belief under discussion embodies a valid argument, although one depending on certain theological assumptions (which are brought out into the open and discussed). It argues, too, that the existence of saintly people is of much more importance than is usually realised, for it is a rare and precious occurrence which requires evaluation and explanation, and one which is relevant to assessing religious truth. It is claimed that if Christianity did not continue to produce saintly people, this would tell against some of its central beliefs, particularly the doctrine of the Holy Spirit.

Patrick Sherry is a Lecturer in the Religious Studies Department at the University of Lancaster. He was educated at the Universities of Oxford, Cambridge and Chicago, and has held visiting appointments in the USA and Canada.

He is the author of *Religion, Truth and Language-Games* and of articles in the *American Philosophical Quarterly, Heythrop Journal, Neue Zeitschrift für Systematische Theologie und Religionsphilosophie, Philosophy, Religious Studies* and *Theology*.

SPIRIT, SAINTS, AND IMMORTALITY

Patrick Sherry

State University of New York Press
Albany

First published in U.S.A. by
State University of New York Press, Albany

For information, address State University of New York
Press, State University Plaza, Albany, N.Y., 12246

Library of Congress Cataloging in Publication Data

Sherry, Patrick.
    Spirit, saints, and immortality.

    Includes bibliographical references and index.
    1. Christian saints.   2. Holiness.   3. Holy Spirit.
4. Image of God.   4. Immortality.   I. Title.
BR1710.S47 1984   235   83–519
ISBN 0–87395–755–5
ISBN 0–87395–756–3 (pbk.)

Printed in Hong Kong

In memory of
my father

Contents

Preface

Many people admire saintliness, but few speculate about its nature and causes. Philosophers tend to treat it, like heroism, as a species of the supererogatory, an interesting but peripheral topic in ethics. Theologians discuss sanctification as a topic in moral theology, or else as an aspect of the theology of the Holy Spirit – a notoriously underdeveloped area of theology, at least in the Western church. Over the last few years I have come to think that the existence of saintly people is of much greater import for theologians than is usually realised, for it raises questions about grace, redemption, the Holy Spirit, the nature of God, the possibility of attaining a likeness to Him and immortality. I mention the last of these topics because saints are believed to have an eschatological significance, both in Christianity, where the indwelling of the Holy Spirit is regarded as a 'first fruits' or 'earnest' of what is to come, and in some other religions which regard their holy men and women as anticipating a future state. One of my particular concerns in this book will be to investigate the nature and grounds of this belief. Moreover, the existence of saints should be considered by philosophers, too, more than it has been, for it is a rare and precious occurrence and one which requires evaluation and explanation. My purpose in this book is to consider some of the philosophical and theological questions raised by the existence of saintly people, concentrating particularly on the connections between the notions of the spirit of God, saintliness, likeness to God and immortality.

I am grateful to my friends and colleagues in Lancaster who have helped me to talk through some of the arguments in this book, and given advice and encouragement, especially Sarah Coakley, who read through and commented on the whole of an earlier draft, and John Clayton and John Rodwell, who did the same with earlier drafts of some of the chapters. Although the book was written in Lancaster, much of the work was done during a year's leave, in which I divided my time between Yale Divinity School and the Theology Department at the University of Notre Dame. I am grateful to Paul Holmer and the Dean, Leander Keck, for inviting me to Yale, and to David Burrell and the President, Fr Theodore Hesburgh, for inviting me to Notre Dame; and to my many friends in both places with whom I discussed this work, particularly Paul Holmer, David Kelsey, Fred Crosson and Gerry Carroll. I would also like to thank Mrs Joan Halstead for her skill in typing, and the editors of the *Heythrop Journal, Neue Zeitschrift für Systematische Theologie und Religionsphilosophie* and *Religious Studies* for letting me use material published in their journals.

University of Lancaster   PATRICK SHERRY

References and Abbreviations

Certain standard abbreviations of the titles of books are used in this work. The most common ones are:

Aquinas
> *C. G. Summa contra Gentiles*
> *S. T. Summa Theologiae*

Barth
> *C. D. Church Dogmatics* (English translation)

Irenaeus
> *Adv. Haer. Adversus Haereses*

Duns Scotus
> *Op. Ox. Opus Oxoniense*

Biblical quotations are usually taken from the Revised Standard Version.

1 Introduction

SPIRITS, SAINTS AND IMMORTALITY

The claim has often been made over the centuries that the presence of the spirit of God is an anticipation of immortality. John Wesley, for instance, says in a sermon:

> The Spirit . . . is some portion of, as well as preparation for, a life in God, which we are to enjoy hereafter. The gift of the Holy Spirit looks full to the resurrection; for then is the life of God completed in us.[1]

Similarly, Karl Barth alludes to the list of the fruit of the Spirit given by St Paul in Galatians v, and says that the limited perfection achieved in this life is the pledge and first fruits of that perfection for which we are destined and which will be manifested when Jesus Christ comes: 'The power of the life to come is the power of his life in this world' (*C.D.* IV. iv. pp.39f). Both he and Wesley point to the link between the presence of the Holy Spirit and sanctification; and this connection is not surprisingly stressed by many Roman Catholic and Orthodox writers who see the saints (by which is not necessarily meant those who have been officially recognised, for example through canonisation; there are always the 'hidden saints') as forerunners of God's Kingdom. Thus Karl Rahner maintains that the church '*must* always have her saints', for she 'is meant to be and to appear as the community of eschatological salvation and of victorious grace'.[2] Similarly, Vladimir Lossky discusses St Maximus 'contention that although the Holy Spirit is present in all Christians, and indeed in all men, he is particularly present in the wisdom and understanding of the saints, and goes on to say:

1

The Church is the sphere within which union with God takes place in this present life, the union which will be consummated in the age to come, after the resurrection of the dead.[3]

The claims made by these writers are, of course, based on certain passages in the New Testament which I shall discuss in Chapter 4, particularly St Paul's statements that the presence of the Holy Spirit is the earnest or first fruits of what is to come. But such claims are not restricted to Christianity, for as we shall see, Judaism also associates the spirit of God with the future life; and many other religions regard their holy men and women as having an eschatological significance. (Saints are also considered by many to have powers of intercession in Heaven, but I shall not discuss this belief here.)

My purpose in this book is to discuss the claim which I have just illustrated mainly, though not exclusively, with reference to Christianity. The claim involves an appeal to three ideas, spirit, saint and anticipation of the life to come, which it connects together. I shall proceed, therefore, by looking at these three ideas and their interconnections; and then by looking at the idea of likeness to God. I need to consider this last idea, because it is implicit in discussion of the others: the Holy Spirit is believed to imprint the likeness of God on men, the saints are said to be renewed in the image of God and therefore more like Him than other people are, and, with regard to the life to come, we are told that 'when He [God] appears we shall be like Him, for we shall see Him as He is' (I Jn iii.2).

SPIRITUALITY, THEOLOGY AND PHILOSOPHY

It remains for me to say something in this introductory chapter about why I am interested in the question I have outlined, and about my method of procedure. Most obviously, the question is an intrinsically interesting and important one, because it concerns both how we live now and the life to come; and it has not been much explored in recent years.

There is, however, a more indirect reason for my concern: my topic of investigation will bring us into three areas of interest, those of spirituality, theology and philosophy. I hope that our investigations may reveal something about the relationship between these three areas.

The term 'spirituality' has become a fashionable one during the last few years, and is often used with a wide range of meaning. I take it that 'spirituality' is simply the noun derived from 'spiritual' and that it usually denotes a concern with the spiritual life; and by 'spiritual life' I understand a way of life in which people attempt to acquire holiness and an awareness of the presence of God through prayer, meditation and other devotional practices.[4] Spirituality is usually thought of as a concern with the inner life, and it is indeed such; but it should not be thought of as *only* a matter of one's inwardness, as a purely private concern, for there is a connection between what is within us and what is revealed and expressed in our outer behaviour – 'by their fruits you shall know them'.[5] Any growth in one's prayer life and awareness of God should be reflected in one's conduct, in some transformation of character (though, typically, such changes are a matter of slow gradual growth).

Spirituality is at the core of any *practice* of a religion. Without prayer and a devotional life a religion becomes mere observance; and without some experience of God's touch it becomes dry and risks death. As F. Crosson says, 'Even if philosophical reason infers the existence of the divine, an inferred God is an absent God. "Dieu sensible au coeur" ... was the way Pascal characterized faith'.[6] If indeed God exists, then we should relate ourselves to Him; and the primary way to do this is through prayer rather than through, say, theological speculation.

I think that the importance of spirituality in the practice of a religion is manifested in many different ways:

(1) Pastorally: one can only really help people (except in cases of, for example, physical pain or financial need) if one has something *within oneself* to give them.

(2) Ecclesiastically: disputes between religious 'progressives' and 'conservatives' may ignore the really important issues and thus encourage the response 'A plague on both your houses!'. The former risk making religious practice a shallow activism if they neglect spiritual formation, whilst the latter risk dwelling too much on the letter of the law, on traditional formulae and practices, without discerning their true purpose.

(3) Ecumenically: G. Curtis suggests that the ecumenical move-

ment may have erred in concentrating too much on the necessity of doctrinal and structural unity among churches, rather than on that element which first won expression and drew veneration in the early centuries – essential holiness.[7] In particular, Western churches have ignored the distinctive contribution of Orthodoxy, which is more in its tradition of spirituality than in its doctrines.

We should also remember the wider ecumenism; spirituality is a concern of non-Christian religions, and may therefore provide a point of contact with them.

(4) Apologetically: traditionally, holiness has been regarded as one of the marks of the church. Readers of von Hügel will have noticed how often he appealed to the holiness of many whom he had encountered in the Roman Catholic Church as a reason for his adherence to that communion.[8] Conversely, John Henry Newman remained in the Church of England in the early 1840s even after he had lost his faith in the theology of the *Via Media* because he thought that it bore the mark of sanctity; he delayed joining the Roman Catholic Church because of 'what I fancied was a fact – the unscrupulousness, the deceit, and the intriguing spirit of the agents and representatives of Rome'.[9]

(5) For understanding religion: a consideration of spirituality is a way of coming to understand many religious concepts like 'grace' and 'salvation', and seeing how they 'latch on' to our experience or, to use a phrase of Ian Ramsey's, how they 'touch down'.[10] Such concepts are, of course, parts of complex theological systems, involving historical, metaphysical and eschatological considerations; but they involve some appeal to men's experience and self-transformation.

The remark of Ian Ramsey's which I have quoted leads us to the wider and more difficult question of the proper relationship between spirituality and theology. It has become something of a commonplace to observe that the two have become separated in recent centuries. Eastern Orthodox writers regard this separation as a feature of Western Christianity (both Catholic and Protestant), which they themselves have largely avoided. They stress that theology must be rooted in a life of prayer, for it is (or should be) an attempt to establish a living relationship with God and not just speculation about His nature. Serge Bolshakoff quotes some remarks made by a monk, Fr Euthemios of Dionysiou:

> One should not try to speculate on theological subjects before his heart is purified. Otherwise he may well fall into error or become an apostate. The Fathers have truly said, 'Every saint is a theologian, and every theologian must be a saint'. It is quite easy to speculate and produce elaborate and seemingly correct systems of thought; living a holy life is a much more difficult task.[11]

Some of the other fathers whom Bolshakoff consulted in his travels stressed the need to start theology from prayer, and remarked on the fact that in the training of Eastern monks there is little study of speculative theology and little use of theology manuals. Rather, theology is absorbed through liturgical texts, through the Scriptures, and through the writings of the Fathers dealing with prayer.

In fact, however, many Western theologians have said similar things in recent decades. Much of the work of Paul Holmer (a Lutheran inspired particularly by Kierkegaard and Wittgenstein) consists of a polemic against those who teach and preach but lack a real understanding of religious practice. He accuses many people, including some philosophers and theologians, of failing to see that we need an acquaintance with the relevant context of speech and action in order to acquire religious concepts, and of confusing religious language with language *about* religion.[12] More specifically, several Anglican and Roman Catholic theologians have commented on the separation between spirituality and theology. Kenneth Leech, for instance, says that 'the study of theology ... cannot survive in a healthy state apart from the life of prayer and the search for holiness ... spirituality is applied doctrine'.[13] Similarly, Thomas Merton writes:

> Contemplation, far from being opposed to theology, is in fact the normal perfection of theology. We must not separate intellectual study of divinely revealed truth and contemplative experience of that truth as if they could never have anything to do with one another. On the contrary they are simply two aspects of the same thing. Dogmatic and mystical theology, or theology and 'spirituality', are not to be set apart ... Unless they

are united there is no fervour, no life and no spiritual value in theology, no substance, no meaning and no sure orientation in the contemplative life.[14]

One of the profoundest recent treatments of the question is in two essays by Hans Urs von Balthasar, 'Theology and Sanctity' and 'Spirituality'.[15] He starts the first of those with a challenging observation: since the great age of scholasticism few theologians have been saints. In earlier centuries the roles of teacher and pastor were usually conjoined, and many of the early Fathers managed to reproduce in their own lives the fullness of the Church's teaching: 'What they taught they lived with such direct-ness . . . that the subsequent separation of theology and spirituality was quite unknown to them' (p.51). But 'As time went on, theology at prayer was superseded by theology at the desk, and this brought about the cleavage now under discussion. "Scientific" theology became more and more divorced from prayer, and so lost the accent and tone with which one should speak of what is holy' (p.85). Mysticism, too, came to be thought of as a set of inner states which we can introspect, with no relation to dogmatic theology: whereas up to the twelfth century 'theologia mystica' was simply dogmatic theology at its profoundest level, whereby we gain an inner understanding of God's revelation and its realisation in the life of faith, hope and charity. Later writers on spirituality, like St Ignatius Loyola and St Francis de Sales, did not succeed in fully relating their work to dogmatic theology: by then ascetical and mystical theology had become separate subjects from dogmatics, and 'the spirituals . . . who sought for an adequate expression of their understanding of revelation, of their contemplation and love of God, found the study of philosophy and theology one long penance' (p.60). Thus spirituality became almost a separate field, and indeed people began to talk in the plural of different spirituali-ties. But for von Balthasar spirituality is, or should be, 'the subjec-tive aspect of dogmatic theology . . . what makes the objective teaching of the church come alive in the individual' (pp.87f).

It would be easy to conclude from all this that spirituality precedes doctrine and theology: *lex orandi lex credendi*. But this is not quite what the writers I have been discussing are saying, nor is it true. It depends what kind of precedence is in question. Histori-cally, it is true that religious practices often ante-date by many years the development of theological speculation and the definition of doctrine: for instance, the practices of praying for the dead and to the saints long preceded the definitions of the doctrines of Purgatory and of the enjoyment of the Beatific Vision by the saints. But *logically*, it is otherwise: worship and other religious practices presuppose certain beliefs, even if some of them are not consciously formulated and therefore are only 'implicit'. People are brought up within religious traditions and learn their spiritual practices through them (even if, as just indicated, traditions continue to develop under the influence of spiritual practice). The writers I have been discussing, however, are not particularly concerned with either historical or logical precedence, but rather with another kind of dependence, which might be described in Wittgensteinian terms as the dependence of language on a 'form of life'. Wittgenstein said that 'To imagine a language means to imagine a form of life' (*Philosophical Investigations*, § 19), and spoke of the tendency of much philosophical language to get cut off from the circumstances which give meaning to our language (ibid, § 116). Now the writers in question are alleging that there is a similar 'idling' in much theological writing and speaking, in that important questions (for example, about the Incarnation or the role of the Holy Spirit) are pursued as intellectual puzzles, or worse, as academic debates, without much reference to the religious context in which these questions first arose or to their relevance for our salvation now.

We have now arrived at some philosophical considerations, and this naturally brings me to my last question, the role of philosophy in our investigation. The pairing of philosophy and spirituality sounds an unlikely one to most contemporary ears; but it is a perfectly reasonable one, given that the area of spirituality raises many important philosophical questions. Moreover, some philo-sophers of distinction have addressed themselves to these questions: much of the recent work of H. H. Price is concerned with them, and in von Hügel we have an example of a man whose whole life was devoted to questions which touched equally on spirituality, theology and philosophy.

If in the spiritual life men claim some experience of God, and if they are changed by this experience and by their practice of prayer and devotion, then this suggests several philosophical questions. The most obvious of them are concerned with religious experience and ethics, and indeed these questions have attracted a wide philosophical literature, even if the word 'spirituality' is rarely used in it. Philosophers in recent decades have been much interested in mysticism and other kinds of religious experience, particularly with regard to its cognitive status. Less commonly, they have raised ethical questions about the value of the ideal patterns which religions lay before us, and about the practices associated with them (for example asceticism). But questions of epistemology and ethics are not the only ones which occur here. There are also questions about language and ontology: the inner and outer transformation aspired to in the religious life is often described in theological terms, for example 'grace', 'sanctification' and 'salvation'. What is the nature of such terms, and why are they used? Are they just, to use a phrase of Paul Edwards', bombastic redescriptions of familiar facts, or do they have an explanatory function? If so, is there any parallel with other 'theory-laden' language, particularly the theoretical language of science? One consideration which arises here is that religious believers regard spiritual changes as being brought about by the agency of a spirit, and may regard them as evidence for its existence. Again, is there any analogy with the appeal to theoretical entities in science? Theists may regard such a comparison as dangerous, since the transcendent and personal character of God differentiates Him from any aspect of the natural world. Yet they also believe that the spirit of God is present in the hearts of men, especially in those who are being sanctified; and indeed that the latter are being renewed in the likeness of God – so presumably some of God's attributes are reflected in them. This in turn raises further questions about the nature of those who are the subjects of divine indwelling, questions of anthropology and psychology. Then there is the question of the relationship between the spiritual transformation achieved in this life, and the life to come.

Even if it were agreed that spirituality is one source of our knowledge of God, we would still face further questions. How does our knowledge of Him gained from this source relate to that derived from other claimed sources, especially Natural Theology and revelation? This is the epistemological side of a related ontological question. What is the relationship between God's various activities: His spirit working within and through our hearts, His working through nature and through history (especially, for Christians, 'salvation history' culminating in the life of Christ)? What is the relationship between creation, redemption and sanctification? The question of God's *actions* raises a related question about His attributes: what properties do we ascribe to Him on theoretical grounds (that is philosophical and theological arguments), and which properties do we ascribe to Him on the basis of religious experience?

I shall not deal with all these questions in this book. I mention them in order to draw attention to the wealth of considerations raised by the existence of the spiritual life. Not all of them are purely philosophical: for instance, since few people today believe that the immortality of the soul can be proved through philosophical argument, any consideration of immortality is likely to take us into theology. But even if one believes in a life after death on theological grounds, one may still ask philosophical questions about such a revealed belief, for instance about the criteria of identity for a resurrected person or disembodied soul.

The particular questions with which I shall deal arise from the claim mentioned at the beginning of this chapter, that the indwelling of the Holy Spirit is a cause of sanctification and a first fruits of the life to come. I will address myself first of all to the question of what such an indwelling is, by considering what is meant by the 'spirit' of God.

2 The Spirit of God

During the last few years there has been a growing concern among Christians with the Holy Spirit, both in the work of professional theologians and in the more popular writings of those involved in the Charismatic Movement. Despite this trend, however, there has been little attempt made recently by philosophers of religion to analyse the concept of a spirit. Of course, there are obvious reasons for this reluctance, stemming mainly from two important trends in recent theology: Bultmann's work on demythologising, and the anxiety of many Christians to avoid a Dualistic account of man. The former has led many Christians to simplify their ontology by rejecting belief in angels, devils and other such spirits as part of an outmoded view of the world. As Bultmann said in a famous passage,

> It is impossible to use electric light and the wireless and to avail ourselves of modern medical and surgical discoveries, and at the same time to believe in the New Testament world of daemons and spirits.[1]

The second consideration, that is the rejection of Dualism, leads Christians to stress that man is a single psycho-physical entity, and not a combination of two substances, body and spirit. This is not to say that talk about the spirit of man is to be rejected; but, following Ryle's treatment of 'mind' in *The Concept of Mind*, it is to be interpreted not as the name of an immaterial substance but as denoting a set of capacities, for example, to reflect on oneself, to make moral judgements, to appreciate or create art, to love and so on. The claim that man is a spirit becomes then perhaps an example of what Wittgenstein called a grammatical remark. I might add that this tendency is not found only amongst philosophers of the Anglo-American analytical tradition. In his *Foundations of Christian Faith* Karl Rahner defines spirit in terms of self-consciousness and self-transcendence: '*spirit* is the single person insofar as he becomes conscious of himself in an absolute presence to himself, and indeed does this by the fact that he is always oriented towards . . . God' (p.183). Elsewhere he attacks what he calls 'platonic spiritualism' for abstracting from the understanding of man as one totality.[2]

This reaction against Dualism also leads Christians to stress that they believe in a resurrection of the *body*, and not in the immortality of a disembodied soul (sometimes, as in the case of Oscar Cullmann, this contrast is made as part of a more general contrast between Hebrew and Greek thought). Such a position does leave us with the awkward question of whether anything survives between death and the resurrection of the glorified body.

Unfortunately there is one kind of spirit which is neither an incarnated spirit, like man's, nor one such as may be easily demythologised away. This is the spirit of God – notice I put it this way, rather than merely saying 'God', for, as we shall see later, it is indeed questionable whether we can simply describe God as a spirit. It is here that the lack of work on the concept of a spirit becomes surprising. My purpose in this chapter will be to do three things: to examine the concept of a divine spirit which is current among contemporary philosophers of religion (both those who think that the concept is coherent and those who dismiss it), to compare it with Biblical usage and to point out certain differences between them, and to consider some of the philosophical and theological issues raised by this comparison. This will, I hope, provide some understanding of what is meant by the indwelling of the Holy Spirit.

SPIRITS AND IMMATERIAL PERSONS

The most common tendency in recent philosophy of religion is simply to define a spirit as a 'person without a body', an 'incorporeal agent', an 'incorporeal personal substance' or some such, and to proceed from there. Thus in his book, *The Coherence of Theism*, Richard Swinburne starts out by defining God as 'something like a person without a body (i.e. a spirit) who is eternal, free, able to do anything, knows everything, is perfectly good . . . the creator and sustainer of the universe' (p.1).[3] In due course there follow chapters on each of the main attributes listed. But very little is said about the concept of a spirit, compared with the other attributes. It is true that there is a long chapter on the concept of an omnipresent spirit (Ch. 7). But most of this chapter consists of a long disquisition on personal identity which Swinburne has previously published elsewhere. As regards the concept of a spirit, Swinburne simply says 'By a "spirit" is understood a person without a body, a non-embodied person' (p.99), without more ado. There is no justification given for this definition, and no discussion of it, for Swinburne launches straight into the task of answering the objections made by Paul Edwards and others to such a concept.

A similar procedure is followed by those who reject the concept of a spirit as incoherent. Paul Edwards, for instance, asks:

> What does it mean to speak of a pure spirit, a disembodied mind, as infinitely (or finitely) powerful, wise, good, just and all the rest?[4]

He argues that we understand such terms when applied to human beings having bodies, with publicly observable behaviour; but we have no idea what it would be like to act justly, for instance, without a body, for 'psychological predicates are *logically* tied to the behaviour of organisms'. This certainly raises an important question about divine agency, but again any further analysis of the concept of a spirit is lacking.

Edwards is content to conclude that the belief that God is a disembodied spirit is unintelligible (p.53). Others have argued that the concept of such a spirit is what might be called an illegitimate reification or hypostatisation: 'spirit' properly refers to certain human capacities, which are abstracted and imagined as existing (in an infinite degree, in the case of God) apart from any physical body, perhaps inhering in an 'immaterial substance'. Antony Flew compares this with Lewis Carroll's Cheshire cat's grin, which is described as still existing when the face disappears.[5]

A second important objection raised by many contemporary philosophers concerns the possibility of identifying a spirit. Antony Flew, for example, claims that it is difficult, if not impossible, to supply appropriate means of identification and criteria of identity for incorporeal personal substances, for the qualification 'incorporeal' negates the identifying content of the term 'substance'.[6]

Swinburne answers these two common objections by arguing that a spirit can express his hopes, fears, wants and so on by intervening in the world, and that in *some* ways God is related to the world as a person to his body; and that personal identity is something ultimate – he accuses Penelhum and others of failing to distinguish two different questions: what does it *mean* to say that person 1 is the same as person 2, and what is the evidence for it (pp.105–10).

We shall have to return to a discussion of these two objections later in this chapter. For the moment, however, I want to concentrate on the definition of a spirit which is assumed without question by both Swinburne and those whom he opposes. Swinburne, as I have said, simply defines a spirit as a 'non-embodied person', by which he means 'an individual who thought and perhaps talked, made moral judgements, wanted this and not that, knew things, favoured this suppliant and not that, etc., but had no body' (p.102). He passes on immediately to discuss the question of what it is to be an omnipresent spirit, and he tackles this in terms of a thought-experiment: we are to imagine ourselves gradually becoming aware of what is happening in other bodies and material objects so that we are able to give invariably true answers to questions about them, coming to see things from any points of view which we choose, able to move directly anything we choose, uttering words which can be heard anywhere, and so on. 'Surely', he concludes, 'anyone can thus conceive of himself becoming an omnipresent spirit' (p.105).

There are a number of things to be said about this account. The spirit described in Swinburne's thought-experiment sounds more like a super-Frankenstein than the God of Abraham, Isaac and Jacob. Now, to be fair, more is said later in the book about the moral and religious attributes of God. But even so, one often feels that 'super-Frankenstein' is merely giving way to Matthew Arnold's 'infinitely magnified Lord Shaftesbury'. No link is made between spirit and spirituality. This, however, is perhaps a personal, religious reaction. A more philosophical objection is that Swinburne nowhere argues for his initial definition of a spirit. Perhaps he thinks that his definition is obviously correct, so that no argument is required. Yet other definitions are possible: for instance, Aquinas at one point says that the rational soul 'is called a spirit according to what properly belongs to itself . . . namely, an immaterial intellectual power' (*S.T.* la. xcvii, 3: this is not his only

definition of spirit). Now such a definition is not incompatible with
Swinburne's; but if we wish to accept both, we require an
argument enabling us to pass from one to the other. The history
of philosophy will suggest many possible arguments. One might
argue that in general a power can only be identified with
reference to a substance or a person, and that it must 'inhere' in
something (I mean other than its recipients); or, more specifically,
one might argue that an intellectual power must inhere in an
intellectual substance,[7] which is personal, if not a person. Or one
might argue that such descriptions are required in order to
explain how spirits can continue to exist when they are not
intervening or dwelling in the world – how they exist on their
days off, as it were. But no such arguments are forthcoming from
Swinburne.

These considerations suggest two different questions:

(1) Has Swinburne defined a spirit correctly?
(2) Is God such a spirit – or, indeed, any kind of spirit?

As regards the first question, Swinburne has some justification for
his position, in that definitions like his have been current in philosophy at least since Locke's time (e.g. *Essay* II. xxiii[8]), and similar
ones are found much earlier (e.g. in Aquinas, *S.T.* Ia.xxxvi.l ad i;
but note that such writers usually prefer to speak of immaterial
substances rather than persons). Moreover, some such definition is
current in ordinary language. People often speak of ghosts, and
indeed the dead generally, as 'spirits'. Such beings are regarded as
incorporeal (at least in the sense of being without ordinary
physical bodies), and as having personal attributes, for example
speaking through mediums, being happy or unhappy, and, in the
case of poltergeists, manipulating material objects (I am not sure
whether this quite makes them 'persons': Strawson has invented
the useful phrase 'former persons' to apply to such cases, a coinage
which has drawn from Flew the sharp comment that 'former
persons . . . are no more a sort of person than ex-wives . . . are a
sort of wives').[9]

Unfortunately, however, the appeals to the history of philosophy and to ordinary language provide insufficient support for
Swinburne's definition. The philosophical tradition running from
scholasticism through Descartes to Locke, Berkeley and others
was already questioned by Hobbes (*Leviathan*, Ch. 34) and later by

Kant when he argued, against Swedenborg, that a spirit should be defined as a being that has reason, for example a man, and not as a separable spiritual substance.[10] Moreover, the appeal to ordinary language is not decisive. Because the term 'spirit' has been used in many different contexts, for example, the Bible, Stoicism, Greek medicine, alchemy, scholastic metaphysics and nineteenth-century Idealism, it has acquired a complex and varied character. Even in everyday parlance it is commonly used in many different ways: we say, for instance, 'There was a spirit of discord there', 'She showed a resolute spirit', 'He took it in the spirit in which it was meant'; we speak too, of the spirit of an age, of a place and of an artistic movement.[11]

Some of these common usages are nearer to the original meaning of the term than later philosophical and theological ones. The Greek *pneuma*, the Hebrew *ruach* and the Latin *spiritus* all meant originally 'breath' or 'wind', and something of this etymological origin survives in ordinary speech and in literature, even in English. The same term was used for 'breath' and 'spirit' because both were thought of as permeating, penetrating or pervading material entities. This is well expressed by Aquinas:

> 'spirit' is taken from the respiration of animals and extended to the impulses and movements of every airy body, e.g. wind or fine vapour diffused through their members for their move-ment; then, because air is invisible, it is extended to all invisible motive powers and substances; and hence to the sensible soul, the angels, the rational soul, and God – God because He proceeds by love, a kind of moving force. (*C.G.* iv.23)

The analogy with 'breath' suggests that we should look a little more closely at the mode of a spirit's action. The words 'permeat-ing', 'penetrating' and 'pervading' which I have mentioned suggest that the workings of a spirit are essentially internal, and particu-larly, in religious contexts, associated with the movement of the heart, with moral awareness, enlightenment and conversion. It is unfortunate, therefore, that so many philosophers of religion look to parapsychology for parallels. Donald Evans, for instance, in his reply to the article by Paul Edwards which I have mentioned, suggests that telepathic influence might provide a model for 'the attitude and initiative of a hidden personal being called "God" '.[12] But since telepathy is normally used to refer to intuitive communication between people distant from each other, this is surely precisely the wrong model for God 'in whom we live and move and have our being'. Similarly with the other commonly used parallel, that of theoretical entities in scientific explanations. The parallel is useful in giving us the idea of an invisible and indepen-dent agent, but it misses the characteristic of *personal* agency. And again, more seriously, it misses, as we shall see shortly, the permeating and moral characteristics of the Holy Spirit, and the link between spirit and spirituality. Wittgenstein said 'Show me how you use the word "spiritual" and I shall see whether the soul is non-corporeal and what you understand by "spirit" ' (*Zettel*, 127). In comparing spirits with poltergeists, electrons and so on we have lost touch with the circumstances in which people begin to speak of the spirit of God (which is not to deny that there may be *some* parallel between them).

Some of these considerations are relevant to the second question which I have raised about Swinburne's account, namely; is God a spirit, of the Swinburnian kind or of any kind? Here, again, there is some support for his position in the history of philo-sophy and theology. The tendency to describe God as a spirit is familiar to us not only from philosophers like Locke, but from classical Christian writers: St Anselm, for example, describes Him as *summus spiritus* (*Monologion*, xxxii), while St Augustine gives a definition not unlike Swinburne's: 'Eternal, immortal, incor-ruptible, unchangeable, living, powerful, beautiful, righteous, good, blessed, spirit' (*On the Trinity*, xv.5).[13] Moreover, the descrip-tion of God as a spirit is scriptural – or is it?

Here I must mention a fact which is perhaps rather surprising: although the Bible often refers to 'the spirit of God', 'the Holy Spirit', and so on, there is no passage which can be taken as straight-forwardly asserting that God is a spirit. The nearest we get to it is in John iv.24[14] which is the remark made by Christ to the woman at the well, translated in the Authorised Version as 'God is a Spirit: and they that worship him must worship him in spirit and truth'. But of course Greek lacks an indefinite article (as indeed does Aramaic),[15] so the beginning of this passage (*pneuma ho Theos*) could equally well be translated as 'God is spirit', and indeed it is so translated by recent versions such as Moffatt, the RSV, NEB and Jerusalem Bible[16]

Such modern translations are in accord with many of the early fathers: Origen, for example, commenting on this passage, adduces the parallels of Deut. iv.24, 'God is a consuming fire', and I John i.5, 'God is light', and argues that such expressions are to be taken figuratively: 'spirit' is used to indicate that God is incorporeal, an intelligent being, and also that He fills us with new life.[17] He accuses Celsus, the pagan opponent of Christianity, of having a materialistic, Stoic conception of spirit (*Cels.* VI.71). Another early Father, Novatian, gives a similar interpretation of John iv.24, and argues that when God is called spirit, this is not meant to be an exhaustive definition of His being, but an attempt to lead on our understanding, as when we call Him Love or Light, though His substance is not contained in either; 'if you take spirit to be the substance of God, you make God out to be a creature, since every spirit is a creature' (*De Trin.* Ch.7; cf. Ch.5). This stricture is directed not against a pagan, but against Tertullian, who not only spoke of spirit as a substance (as it were, the kind of stuff of which God is made), but asserted that since God is spirit, He is [a] body, for spirit is body of a kind (*Adv.Prax.* 7;27). Novatian was one of many early Fathers who was chary of using pagan, particularly Stoic, concepts in theology.

THE BIBLICAL WITNESS

Since I have raised the question of how modern philosophical treatments of the divine spirit are related to the Biblical evidence, let me go on to say a little more about the latter. In the Bible the term *pneuma* is used very widely: of God's spirit, of angels and evil spirits, of men or some aspect of man, of departed spirits, and of course in its original senses of breath and wind.[18] Since I have neither the time nor the expertise to attempt a complete account of 'the Biblical concept of spirit' (if there is such a thing), let me restrict myself to looking at some uses of the term as applied to the spirit of God or the Holy Spirit and to pointing out three characteristics which distinguish them. The spirit of God is seen as a *power*, a power which *permeates* the world, especially men, and one which, when permeating men, is particularly associated with *the heart* (in the Biblical sense of the inner person, the seat of reason as well as of the will and of the emotions, which is aware of God's presence and determines conduct). Let me say a little more about each of these characteristics.

Power. Geoffrey Lampe argues[19] ' "spirit" properly refers, not to

God's essence but to his activity, that is to say, his creativity' (p.17). He goes on to point out that the term should be related to others like 'angel', 'hand', 'power', and 'wisdom', terms which, when used of God, refer to His action as discerned in the affairs of men. In the case of spirit, this activity takes many and varied forms: in the Old Testament creation is the work of God's spirit – and here there is often a play on the original meaning of *ruach* and *pneuma*, that is wind or breath (Gen. ii.7; Ps xxxiii.6; civ.30; Job xxxiv.14);[20] but usually more specific things are attributed to its work: Samson's extraordinary physical strength (Judges xiv.6), the skill, perception and knowledge of a craftsman, Bezalel (Ex. xxxv.31), Saul's ecstasy (I Sam. x.6), and prophetic inspiration (Num. xi.25; Ezek. xi.5; Joel iii.1; Si. xlviii.24); when David was anointed by Samuel, the spirit of God seized on him (I Sam. xvi.13). In the later books of the Old Testament more attention is given to the moral and religious character of the spirit's endowments: God's spirit brings wisdom, counsel and sanctity (Is. xi.1f; Wis. vii.7; ix.17); it gives men a new spirit and removes the heart of stone (Ezek. xxxvi. 26f), creating a clean heart (Ps li.10f); it brings a message of justice and good news to the poor (Is. xlii.1; lxi.1).

Many of these endowments continue to be spoken of in the New Testament: St Paul's list of 'gifts of the Spirit' includes preaching, teaching, faith, healing, working miracles, prophecy, discerning spirits, speaking in tongues and administering (I Cor. xii.8-11; Rom. xii.6-8). His 'fruit of the Spirit' refers more to aspects of the human character, love, joy, peace and so on (Gal. v.22; Rom. xiv.17). In addition, the Holy Spirit is given the particular role of 'the Comforter' (or 'Counsellor'), who will remain with the Apostles and lead them to a deeper knowledge of Christ's teaching (Jn xiv.16f; 26; xvi.7f; 13; Acts ix.31). The Spirit is depicted in Acts as guiding the early Church, giving it spiritual strength and a discernment of God's will. St Paul also speaks of the Spirit as 'leading' men, as inspiring prayer and as the source of new life and resurrection (Rom. viii.14; 26f; 11; I Cor. xv.45).

Now in all these cases God's spirit is seen as a power which endows men with new abilities, sometimes temporarily (as in the case of Samson or the prophets), sometimes permanently – unless men quench the Spirit – as in the case of moral and religious attributes. The word 'power' is often used in the same context, whether of the power of the Spirit himself (Lk. i.35; Rom. xv.13), or of the power which the Spirit brings to men (Micah iii.8; Acts i.8; cf. also Si. lviii.24; Lk. iv.14).[21] Another description often used is that of being *given* (e.g. Lk. xi.13; Acts ii.38; Rom. v.5; I Thess. iv.8), to indicate that the power of the Spirit is not at one's own disposal and that its source is outside (we shall have to look later at what the inside/outside contrast is here).

Permeation. Although the power is regarded as coming from outside, it is described as 'filling', 'penetrating' and 'living in' creation or mankind (Wis. i.7, vii.23; Eph. v.18; James iv.5). Again, the etymological link with the concept of 'breath' plays an important role here. Although miracles and extraordinary powers are attributed to the Spirit on occasion, part of its function is to uphold the ordinary laws of nature. It is misguided therefore, of Bultmann to talk of the Spirit as if it were a kind of 'spanner in the works', as it were, when he says: 'Biological man cannot see how a supernatural entity like the *pneuma* can penetrate within the close texture of his natural powers and set to work within him'.[22] One might as well ask how encouragement, friendship and words of advice manage to penetrate biological entities. The problem only arises if you have a crudely Physicalistic view of man. Bultmann's crudity here is surprising, for elsewhere he shows a sensitive understanding of the way in which the penetration of the Holy Spirit differs from that of some magic power: he points out that in the New Testament the Spirit's might is not a magical or mechanical power but one which demands and presupposes a transformation of the will, one which is received by the heart.[23] But this takes me to my third attribute.

The Heart. The Psalmist prays 'God, create a clean heart in me.do not deprive me of your holy spirit' (Ps li.10f; cf. Ezek. xi.19). We find that New Testament writers often speak of the Spirit as being located in men's hearts (e.g. Rom. v.5; II Cor. i.22; Gal. iv.6) and as leading to wisdom and understanding (I Cor. ii.12-15; xii.8) and to works of love (Gal. v.22): St Paul says 'may he [the Father] give you the power through his Spirit for your hidden self to grow strong, so that Christ may dwell in your hearts through faith, and then, planted in love and built on love . . .' (Eph. iii.16f). The presence of the Spirit is seen as essentially linked, too, with repentance, prayer and faith (Acts ii.38; Rom. viii.15f): this again would seem to distinguish it from a magical power, as perhaps also does the fact that the Spirit may be 'quenched' or 'suppressed' (I Thess. v.19).

The fact that the Spirit is linked to the heart does not, I think, entail that it must always be consciously experienced. It is true that it is sometimes associated in the New Testament with men's inwardness (e.g. in I Cor. ii.10f), an association which plays an important role in German Idealism and in theology influenced by it (e.g. Karl Rahner). But it is also associated with those changes of character which are described as 'sanctification' or 'the fruit of the Spirit'. Such changes are often brought about only gradually: we must not therefore, I think, exclude the possibility of a spirit acting without our being conscious of its operations, so that its power is known through its effects.[24]

How does my characterisation of certain uses of the Biblical concept of spirit relate to Swinburne's concept? In the book I have mentioned, *God as Spirit*, Lampe notes that in the early Church the term 'spirit' tended to lose its traditional connotation of 'activity', and instead was used to denote the divine being; as he puts it, it becomes in the early Fathers 'an ontological rather than a functional term' (p.210). I have already described how this tendency continued in later philosophy, and it would seem that Swinburne and other philosophers stand at the end of a long tradition. But what exactly is the difference between the two concepts?

Swinburne, as we have seen, defines a spirit as a 'non-embodied person', whilst other philosophers, for example Locke and Berkeley, have talked rather of immaterial substances. These definitions say both more and less than the Biblical usage. They say less because they forget that 'spirit' is a metaphor in origin and because they do not do justice to the three characteristics which I have just outlined; they say more, in that they go beyond the Bible in describing a spirit as a 'substance' or a 'person'. This is not to say that such descriptions are incorrect, or that they are incompatible with the Biblical descriptions; but we do require an argument to move from one to the other. There are two possibilities here, philosophical and theological. The first is to use the kind of argument which I mentioned earlier with reference to Descartes, and to say that power must inhere in a substance, and that a spiritual power must inhere in an immaterial substance (or person). The second is to argue that spirits are persons because we describe them in terms appropriate to personal beings. Although it is true that, as one commentator notes, neither Hebrew nor Greek have words corresponding to 'person' or 'personal' with their modern connotations,[25] and that the Trinitarian term *prosōpon* is to be taken in a special sense, nevertheless it is the case

that the Holy Spirit is often called the Counsellor or the Comforter, and the New Testament speaks of him as giving birth,
speaking, teaching, witnessing, helping, leading and generally
guiding the early Church (e.g. Jn iii.6; xiv.26; xvi.13; Acts viii.29;
x.19; xiii.2-4; xvi.6; xx.23; Rom. viii.16, 26), all of which are terms
normally used of persons. Moreover, John xvi.8, 13-15 uses the
masculine form *ekeinos* to refer to the Spirit, even though the term
pneuma is neuter. The responses of men to the Spirit, too, are
described in terms used of responses to a person: lying, putting to
the test, grieving (Acts v.3, 9; Eph. iv.30; Is. lxiii.10). But it needs to
be noted that this kind of language is accompanied by impersonal
language; the Spirit is 'poured out' and 'given to men to drink',
whilst men are 'filled' by it or may 'quench' it (Is. xliv.3; Lk. i.67;
Acts ii.4, 33; x.45; I Cor. xii.13; Eph. v.18, I Thess. v.19).[26] Granted
that some of this is metaphorical language (as, of course, is 'spirit'
itself originally), it is nevertheless not language which is naturally
appropriate to a person.[27]

So much for the differences between the two concepts. Now, in
what respects are they alike? Firstly, they are both said to be
immaterial or incorporeal. Isaiah contrasts 'spirit' with 'flesh'
when he says 'the Egyptian is a man, not a god; his horses are
flesh, not spirit' (xxxi.3; cf. Jn iii.6; it should be noted, however,
that the New Testament contrast between 'flesh' and 'spirit' is
often used more to make an ethical than an ontological point: see
Isaacs, *The Concept of Spirit*, Ch.8). Secondly, the different terms
'power' and 'person' both indicate that a spirit exists independently of men and has causal efficacy. This is an important point,
for it goes against the common tendency to see a spirit as the
projection of spirit, understood as certain human capacities. This
tendency is exemplified in Ian Crombie's influential article, 'The
Possibility of Theological Statements'.[28] There he defines a spirit as
'a being outside space and time', and says that we conceive of such
a notion from concepts like loving, feeling and hoping which are
applied to human beings but which are relatively independent of
space. He goes on to say that such a notion is illegitimate, for it is a
'reified abstraction', formed by moving from the abstract noun
'spirit' to the common noun 'a spirit'. But this gives far too much
away, as critics have not been slow to point out.[29] For if spirit
properly denotes a set of human capacities, then not only is
Crombie abusing language but his God may turn out to be like the
Cheshire cat's smile. But Crombie has ignored the history of the

concept, particularly its Biblical roots and its etymology. Again, let me repeat that for Biblical writers much talk about spirits is causal: men who are filled with the Spirit have new capacities, yes indeed, but they regard them as being caused by something outside of themselves, a power, and so see them as a gift (this power is described in anthropomorphic language, but that is another question). The power is called a spirit — often 'the Holy Spirit'. People may be wrong in thinking that there are immaterial forces at work within them; nevertheless, that is what the term 'spirit' often *means*.[30]

SPIRIT, ACTION AND IDENTIFICATION

In this chapter I have been examining the kind of definition of a spirit which is accepted without question by many modern philosophers, and I have pointed out that it is inadequate if it is taken as a full account of what the term means. But suppose we adopt an alternative definition, such as 'a non-physical power permeating creation, particularly men's hearts'. Where does this leave the philosophical problems raised at the beginning of this chapter?

I think that providing an alternative definition neither answers the objections nor renders them wholly irrelevant, but that it does shift the area of debate somewhat. The kind of alternative definition which I have suggested is not only one which is closer to Biblical usage and to the etymology of the terms *ruach, pneuma* and *spiritus* but also one which has some grounding in experience (whereas 'immaterial substances' or 'non-embodied persons' sound more like inferred entities whose existence is known through Natural Theology). The starting-point is the experience of being 'empowered' in the ways I have described, and this leads men to ascribe their new capacities to an external cause, partly because they think that they have not acquired them by their own efforts and cannot do so, partly because they sometimes feel conscious of the workings of this power. Thus Keith Ward says of the Holy Spirit that it is 'a force arising within individuals, yet somehow other than them'.[31]

Clearly, however, these considerations do not evade philosophical problems. People may think that they experience a power within them, but it may just be that they can do more than they know, that they have underdeveloped capacities. So what reason is there to hypothesise an external cause, let alone a cause of *this* kind, a spirit? Is not such a move from talk of human capacities to talk of a spirit an example of what William James called an 'over-belief'? In any case, what is the inside/outside distinction here?

One answer I have suggested is that the capacities attributed to a spirit's power and gift are not under one's own control. But then many ordinary physical states, like feeling tired, energetic, well or ill are not usually under our control either. In any case, is talk of 'non-physical powers' acting in various ways any better off than talk of 'non-embodied persons'? Does it not still involve an illegitimate hypostatisation? What does it mean to say that such powers are wise and loving, that they lead or teach men? Moreover, how would we identify them – how would I tell that I was empowered by the Holy Spirit rather than by Satan or the Muses?

These questions amount to a rephrasing of the objections raised by Edwards, Flew and Nielsen which I mentioned at the beginning of this chapter. Let me comment on some of them separately.

First *action and language*. It is tempting to claim that the phrase 'non-physical' power is nonsensical, for power is the transference of physical energy. But this is over-simple, and does not do justice to the variety of our usage. Often when we use the phrase 'physical force' we make a contrast (explicitly or implicitly) with the power of rationality and language, as for instance when we say 'he got his way not by brute force but by the power of his words' (or his intellect or reasoning). This contrast is well brought out by Jung when he contrasts the treating of neuroses by means of drugs with psychotherapy. He says:

> A suitable explanation or a comforting word to the patient may have something like a healing effect . . . The doctor's words, to be sure, are 'only' vibrations in the air, yet . . . the words are effective only in so far as they convey a meaning or have signifi-cance. It is their meaning which is effective. But 'meaning' is something mental or spiritual. Call it a fiction if you like. None the less it enables us to influence the course of the disease in a far more effective way than with chemical preparations.[32]

It might be replied that this is a poor parallel, since counselling is still a transaction between two physically embodied persons, doctor and patient. But this is to miss the point, that such a transaction is something more than a transfer of energy, for it involves *meanings*.

Of course, one can believe in communication through language (and painting or music) without wanting to speak of spirits. I am suggesting only that such a communication gives us a good starting-point for trying to grasp the idea of a non-physical power, one that is as good as that from parapsychology and better than that from theoretical entities in science, for it gives us the concept of an interaction which is not a crude 'spanner in the works' process (which is why I prefer terms like 'permeation', 'penetration' and 'pervading' to 'interaction', although the last is commonly used of spirits).

Another advantage of using this starting point is that it enables us to meet Paul Edwards' objection, about the propriety of applying predicates like 'wise', 'good', 'just 'and 'powerful' to an incorporeal spirit. For we already use such terms of human expressions and creations which communicate meanings, as when we speak of a 'powerful argument', 'moving words', 'a thoughtful book' or 'an intelligent film'. It may be replied that these are analogical uses: I am not sure that all of them are, but even if they are, this is sufficient to refute the objection that they may be used only of bodily organisms. Thus if certain happenings were brought about by the help or the teaching of the Holy Spirit, if certain human characteristics were his fruit or gifts, then it would be correct to ascribe terms like those mentioned by Edwards to him. Clearly, however, we could only justify such ascriptions if we could identify the actions of this or any other spirit: and this takes us on to the second main problem raised at the beginning of this chapter, that of identification.

Identification. Even though I have adopted a different definition of a spirit from Flew (and Swinburne), a problem of identification[33] still remains: in the present case it is that of knowing what would constitute good grounds for the claim that different people are empowered or influenced by the same spirit.

At the practical level spiritual directors and religious superiors are sometimes faced with the task of 'discerning' spirits, or, as one might put it, of detecting 'spiritual phoneys'. The early Church set out three criteria, namely ethical, communitarian and Christological: those called upon to discern looked for God-like characteristics, for the 'fruit of the Spirit', since the Lord who is Spirit turns men into images of Him (II Cor. iii.18); for unity, because the one Spirit which all believers share creates fellowship (Phil. ii.i; II Cor.

xiii.14);[34] and for an acknowledgement of Christ ('You can tell the spirits that come from God by this: every spirit that acknowledges that Jesus the Christ has come in the flesh is from God; but any spirit which will not say this ... is the spirit of Antichrist' – 1 Jn iv.2f; cf. 1 Cor. xii.3).

Now clearly these criteria of discernment are internal to Christianity; and they assume that there are non-physical powers, of which the good must be distinguished from the bad. But what if one were to object, as I think Flew and Nielsen would do, that we can only identify spatio-temporal particulars, and that the early Church was sorting out good and bad *people*, not spirits? The kind of identification in question is not that of telling whether something is the same particular, but rather that of telling if it is the same *sort* of thing or quality – in this case, whether someone shows the desired Christian characteristics.

There are a number of things to be said here. First of all, we must distinguish between first and third person accounts. Someone who is trying to discern the consciously felt presence of the Holy Spirit in himself or herself is not trying to identify a spatio-temporal particular, but to judge the nature and provenance of an experience. As regards other people, it is perfectly true that the early Church, in testing spirits, was indeed judging people or rather certain aspects of people; but again, it saw these as subject to outside influences. Similarly, when people today speak of the guidance of the Holy Spirit, they do not usually claim to identify Him *per se*: what they do is to identify an impulse or prompting of the heart in themselves, or some actions, words or dispositions of character in others, and say '*That* is the working of the Holy Spirit'. In other words, causal claims are being made. But such causal claims are not simply inductions to efficient causes, as when we say things like 'It must be Mary who made that mess in the kitchen; she always leaves things in a shambles': I think that if they were, we should be regarding spirits simply as invisible persons (like Gyges in Plato's *Republic*, Bk. II) – precisely the tendency I have been attacking. Rather, they are also somewhat similar to claims like 'That statue has only one arm because it's a statue of Nelson', which are claims about what Aristotle called formal causes; and also to the claims we make when we identify works of art, and also theories, arguments and so on. What happens is that we read something or hear a particular musical performance, and in them we recognise a particular theory, argument, plot, symphony or whatsoever. Now admittedly the particular instantiation is a spatio-temporal particular; for the entities I have mentioned are 'incarnated' in material objects like books, scores and gramophone records, and they are communicated by material means like printing, vocal cords and musical instruments. But this does not mean that they are identical with them: Homer's poems existed before they were ever written down, for they were transmitted by word of mouth, and one can imagine a piece of music (for example a banned national anthem) which was never recorded or transcribed in scores but was passed down from one group of performers to another.

The parallel which I have again drawn with works of art is, I repeat, only a partial one, used here to show that identification is not always a straight-forward matter of picking out an object or a person. In the case of works of art we regard a spatio-temporal particular as exemplifying something, for example a symphony, which is identified through it. In the case of spirits the religious believer claims to identify a common source of certain powers in men. This source (unlike a work of art) is regarded as an agent, partly for the reasons already mentioned, especially the experience of power, partly for other theological reasons which lead people to identify this power with the spirit of God or the Holy Spirit.

IMMATERIAL SUBSTANCES AND PERSONS

It remains for me to say a little more about these theological reasons, and also about philosophical definitions of a spirit in terms of an immaterial substance or person. I can imagine the following objection being put to me at this point: 'You have said what the word "spirit" means in terms of the kind of experiences of power which give rise to spirit-talk. But you have not said what spirits are *in themselves*. Now if they are not immaterial substances or persons, then what are they?'

I take it that this objection is saying more than that to the substantive 'spirit' there must correspond a substance or person. Such an argument is invalid and has been much criticised in the last few decades, for instance in Gilbert Ryle's *The Concept of Mind*. Rather, the objection is saying that even if the term 'spirit' means a power of a certain sort, still we cannot evade the task of giving an account of the ontological status of such a power. It must inhere in something, or be the power of something; and if we are unwilling to say that it can be reduced to some aspect of the human personality, then it must be an immaterial agent. Of course, one who experiences the influence of such a power may be hard put to give an account of its ontological status: nevertheless it is incumbent on the philosopher to try to do so.

The term 'immaterial substance' needs looking at carefully. It arouses suspicion among philosophers today, though this was not always so. The stranger in Plato's *Sophist* suggests that the power to change or to be changed, rather than materiality, constitutes real being (247D–E). Aquinas devoted much attention to 'intellectual substances' and 'subsisting forms', especially angels (he used the term 'spirit' relatively rarely of them, as I have already noted). Of course, he realised that even in the ancient world many thinkers were opposed to the notion that the world is peopled with immaterial entities: in *C.G.* II.91 he cites the Sadducees and some ancient philosophers as having believed that every substance is corporeal, and Origen as having believed that God is the only bodiless substance. Hobbes dismissed the idea of an 'incorporeal substance' as being an absurd use of language, for one term cancels out the other (*Leviathan*, Chs 5, 34. This is not to say that he opposed the notion of a spirit: in his response to Dr Bramhall he said that God 'is a most pure, and most simple corporeal spirit', and defined spirit, curiously, as 'thin, fluid, transparent, invisible body' (*Works*, ed. Molesworth, IV, pp. 306, 309)). Hume, too, rejected the idea of an immaterial substance in his *Dialogues on Natural Religion* VI,[35] and in his *Treatise on Human Nature* I.iv.5. In the latter he rejected the view that our perceptions must inhere in an immaterial substance, the soul, on the grounds that we have no impression of such a substance and cannot envisage how an unextended substance could be joined with an extended one, and that anyway perceptions can exist separately, without inhering in anything. But Hume should not be labelled a Materialist since he said that 'an object may exist and yet be nowhere', and noted that moral reflections, passions and sentiments have no location. His purpose was merely to attack the claim that such things must inhere in an immaterial substance. He did not follow thorough-going Materialists like La Mettrie and his successors in wishing to reduce all thoughts and sensations to physical processes.

My own view is that 'immaterial substance' is not a particularly

helpful phrase: it is mainly a negative description which serves to
rule out certain possibilities, namely that whatever is in question is
a material object or an aspect of something else, or that it exists
only intermittently. 'Immaterial' is a negative term, used to
describe entities of which it does not make sense to ask questions
about size, weight, colour and so on (of course, we do not ask such
questions about abstractions, either). 'Substance' is more difficult
to analyse. Probably most people would think of a spiritual
substance in Lockean terms, as 'a something I know not what' in
which spiritual powers inhere. But this does not get us very far.
And if we think of it as a body or a kind of 'stuff', we encounter
Hobbes' objection that the terms 'incorporeal' and 'substance'
contradict each other.[36] It will, I think, be more helpful in the
present context to take the term as simply indicating that what is
in question exists continuously and independently (in the sense
that it does not exist in something else, as attributes do).[37] Thus in
saying that a spirit is an immaterial substance (or, better, that it is
the power of such a substance), we are allowing the latter a
continuous and independent existence, and denying that it is a
material object or an aspect of some other being.

Some of these considerations apply to the other common
definition of a spirit given nowadays, namely a 'disembodied
person'. I have already argued at some length that the two terms
did not originally have the same meaning, even if they are now so
regarded (as Wittgenstein says 'when our language suggests a
body and there is none: there, we should like to say, is a *spirit*' (*P.I.*
36)); I have also drawn attention to our natural tendency to
imagine a disembodied person as an invisible man, like Gyges.
Nevertheless, it may be objected that, ontologically speaking, a
spirit *is* a disembodied person. This may well be so. But we must
ask exactly what this claim amounts to and what grounds there
are for making it. It would seem that the term 'disembodied' is a
negative one, like 'immaterial'; and that 'person' goes beyond
'substance' in drawing attention to the belief that spirits act, and
their actions are regarded as analogous to those of embodied
persons, in that they manifest intelligence, purpose, love and so
on. Now since, if I am right, 'spirit' does not *mean* 'disembodied
person' (as a character in Bernard Malamud's novel *The Fixer* says,
'A force is not a father'), we require some reasons for equating the
two. I have already suggested some possible philosophical and
theological lines of argument. But I suspect that people's belief in

personal spirits is more often based on experience than on arguments. Such experiences might include both a sense of the presence or activity of a spiritual power and a period of reflection in which people discern a pattern in their lives analogous to the recurrent and recognisable characteristics of the work of a personal being. Thus John V. Taylor says that people use personal language of the power of the Holy Spirit because its effect is always to foster new personal responses and relationships:

> In every encounter there has been an anonymous third party who makes the introductions, acts as a go-between, makes two beings aware of each other, sets up a current of communication between them. What is more, this invisible go-between does not simply stand between us, but is activating each of us from the inside. (*The Go-Between God*, p.17)

This describes very well the kind of experiences which lead people to regard a spirit as a person. Nevertheless, it also suggests that this claim is not something which one could read straight off from the relevant experiences, but is something that follows reflection. So the statement that a spirit is a disembodied person is not to be accepted as an initial definition, but more as an inference.

This point applies even more to the claim that the power which someone experiences is the Holy Spirit or the spirit of God. This is not something one could simply 'read off' from the experience of being empowered, but it is an interpretation based on reflection on one's own experiences and on the religious tradition in which one stands. For one could not tell simply from being empowered that the spirit empowering one was of a being who is almighty, all-knowing, infinitely good, creator of the universe, and so on. I think that this is a case where John Hick's notion of 'experiencing as' is applicable.[38] James Dunn sees such a process of interpretation occurring in Jesus' mind:

> 'Spirit of God' in Judaism denoted the power of God which could take hold of a man and inspire him to act as God's prophet in word and deed . . . *Jesus' consciousness of spiritual power* . . . was an *awareness* of otherly power working through him, together with the *conviction* that this power was *God's* power.[39]

Moreover, says Dunn, the exercise of this power was evidence for Jesus that the Kingdom of God had already come (Mt. xii.28).

The role of interpretation in talk about the Spirit is taken a stage further when people come to speak of the Holy Spirit as a 'person' (in the sense of *prosōpon* or *hypostasis*) in the Trinity. This is the sort of statement that is based on long theological reflection; and, as a matter of history, it was reached only after about two centuries of such reflection, and not defined as doctrine until the following century. Yet a further stage of theorising was reached when particular theologies of the Trinity and the roles of the Persons within it were elaborated, for instance St Augustine's view, subsequently so influential in the West, that the Holy Spirit is the bond of love between Father and Son. It would be outside the scope of this chapter to discuss the reasons for these developments, although clearly the doctrine owes much both to experiential considerations which I shall touch on in Chapter 5 and to some of the passages from Scripture already mentioned, for example St Paul's Trinitarian formula in II Cor. xiii.14 or Christ's promises to send the Holy Spirit as recorded in the Fourth Gospel's account of his discourse at the Last Supper (similarly, St Augustine appealed to Rom. v.5 in support of his view).[40] Suffice it to say that both the doctrine and the theologies arose out of a desire to relate to each other God's being Creator and Father, His incarnation in Jesus Christ, and His presence as inspirer and sanctifier. It is the third of those which is my concern in this book. My next task, therefore, is to extend our understanding of what the spirit of God is by studying more closely the phenomena which are particularly ascribed to His action. I shall do this now by looking at the notion of sanctification.

3 Saints

Since the early centuries of the Church it has been common to link holiness and sanctification particularly with the Holy Spirit. St Basil, for instance, describes the Holy Spirit as 'a living substance, having the power of sanctification', for whom 'holiness is the complement of His nature'.[1] Such an association had already been made in the New Testament (e.g. Rom. xv.16, I Pet. i.2); and one of the few references in the Old Testament to the *holy* spirit of God associates it with a clean heart (Ps li.10f). My purpose in this chapter is to discuss the nature of sanctity and its religious significance, and then to consider certain philosophical problems which it raises, especially with regard to its causes. I shall argue that there are *some* similarities between religious explanations of sanctification and scientific explanations (as well as some dissimilarities), and that the phenomenon of sanctity has an evidential value.

THE RELIGIOUS SIGNIFICANCE OF SANCTITY

The term 'holy' nowadays tends to have almost purely ethical connotations. The biblical term *qadosh*, however, originally had a much richer depth of meaning than this, for holiness was ascribed to people (and to places, sacred vessels and so on) in virtue of being set apart in a relationship to God: 'For I am the Lord your God. Consecrate yourselves therefore, and be holy, for I am holy' (Lev.xi.44; cf. xix. 2; xx.8). Nevertheless, the biblical concept *includes* a strongly ethical component,[2] for the Old Testament links holiness with righteousness. The instruction 'You shall be holy; for I the Lord your God am holy' in Leviticus xix, 2 is immediately followed by a series of ethical prescriptions about honesty, respecting parents, protecting the poor and the stranger, and so on. Isaiah says that God will display His holiness by His righteousness

31

(v.16), and Jeremiah depicts God addressing the land of Judah as a 'habitation of righteousness' and a 'holy hill' (xxxi.23). Similarly, the New Testament shows the Holy Spirit as causing many of the ethical qualities associated with our ordinary-language concept of 'saintliness', especially the nine described as the 'fruit of the Spirit': love, joy, peace, patience, kindness, goodness, faithfulness, gentleness and self-control (Gal. v.22f).

The New Testament sometimes ascribes the term 'holy' to Christians simply in virtue of being Christians (for example in I Cor. vii,14), because of their dedication to God and adoption by Him; but in other passages holiness is spoken of more as a duty or a goal, for example in I Thess. iv.3-8 and Heb. xii.14. The *Epistle of Barnabas* speaks beautifully of the 'pilgrimage towards holiness' in the 'companionship of the Lord' (§1)[3]. If one thinks that sanctification, for Christians, is a matter of acquiring the fruit of the Spirit and thereby becoming Christ-like and God-like, then, typically, this is a slow process. Usually it takes a whole lifetime, for the process is one of slow growth, of gradual changes in behaviour which may result eventually in an inner and outer remaking. It involves effort, but is distinguished from any secular technique of self-transformation or self-cultivation in being ascribed to God's grace. As von Hügel puts it:

> God is as truly the source of gradual purification as of sudden conversion, and as truly the strength which guards and moves us straight on, as that which regains and calls us back.[4]

If the process of sanctification is usually a long and slow one, we may often be unaware of God's help in it; for people may be helped without realising it at the time and without any awareness of the presence of a helper (hence we must distinguish the *activity* of the Holy Spirit from the sense of his presence). The existence of the helper and the nature of the help is often discerned only much later, when people look back on the span of their lives and put things into a perspective. Of course there may be some high points or 'peaks' in the process, some distinctive religious experiences, perhaps. But, again, they must not be viewed in isolation.

Thus Aelred Squire says:

> But what interests St. Bernard is experience seen in a context. Tremendously important for our general spiritual develop-

ment, and also for our life of prayer, is the capacity to get a sense of ourselves as persisting through a whole succession of happenings.[5]

Whether or not there are high points in the process, and whether or not the subject is aware of what is happening, I take it that the kind of self-transformation denoted by the term 'sanctification' is something which is usually visible to others, including non-religious people, in that the fruit of the Spirit involves overt behaviour (of course, the inner life of prayer, the acceptance of suffering and so on which lie behind them are not apparent to the casual observer). What is distinctive to religious people is, not that they alone see and admire the process, but that they draw it into a wider range of theological concepts and explanation.

This tendency to fit the phenomenon of sanctity into a theological scheme is shown by the way in which right from the start Christians have given their own religious interpretation to it. Most simply, the Gospels speak of 'change of heart' (*metanoia*) or 'rebirth' as marks of discipleship. Similarly, St Paul speaks in bold language of 'newness of life' (Rom. vi.4), 'a new creation' (Gal. vi.15) and then of 'Christ being formed in you' (Gal. iv.19) and 'a new nature, created after the likeness of God in true righteousness and holiness' (Eph. iv.24; cf. Col. iii.10). For him, as for many others, sanctity is one aspect of an all-demanding relationship with Christ. Moreover, the last two quotations show how the remaking of man has already become subject to theological interpretation. St Paul sees the sanctified as embodying Christ's attributes, as he embodies those of God, while St Peter goes a step further and even speaks of men's sharing in the divine nature (II Pet i.4). This last reference is one source of the concept of *theōsis* (a term better translated as 'divinisation', rather than 'deification' and used nowadays more by Eastern Orthodox than Western theologians).

More specifically, the transformation of man is related to particular doctrines. We have already noticed how it is regarded as the work of the Holy Spirit. But it is also seen as the harvest of Christ's redemption and a mark of those who will inherit his Kingdom (Rom. vi.22; I Cor. vi.9–11), and, as we shall see in the next chapter, it is regarded as a first fruits and an earnest of our future inheritance. We shall see, too, in Chapter 5, how theologically important the theme of 'likeness to God' is: this is a notion derived by St Paul and other early Christian writers from their *milieu*, and adapted by being particularly applied to Christ, 'the very image of God' (II Cor. iv.4); but it is also applied to men who, in being sanctified, are drawn into a closer likeness to God. St Paul speaks of those whom God has called as being 'conformed to the image of his son, in order that he might be the first-born among many brethren' (Rom. viii.29). The second Vatican Council brings together the two themes of likeness to God and the eschatological significance of sanctity when it says:

> When we look at the lives of those who have faithfully followed Christ, we are inspired with a new reason for seeking the city which is to come. . . . In the lives of those who shared in our humanity and yet were transformed into especially successful images of Christ (cf. II Cor. iii.18), God visibly manifests to men His presence and His face. He speaks to us in them, and gives us a sign of His kingdom to which we are powerfully drawn.[6]

In drawing attention to the attractive and inspiring character of sanctity this passage suggests another, more practical point: for many people meeting a saintly person is a religious experience and may even lead to a religious conversion. This is not necessarily because of what the saint says, but because of what he *is*. Thus Henri de Lubac writes:

> But let a saint come on the scene . . . and the miracle happens again. 'These times', the Abbé Monchanin confided, 'people have said that they sense God through me . . .' So it was yester-day – and so it will be tomorrow. The veil is suddenly rent . . . when a saint passes, it is a call to conversion.[7]

Why do the saints (by which, again, I do not necessarily mean those who have been officially recognised) sometimes have this effect? Of course, the qualities of love, gentleness and so on are immediately attractive to most people, particularly when they are accompanied by joyfulness (von Hügel said that Pope Benedict XIV's stipulation that there should be a note of joy in the lives and influence of those put forward for canonisation was nothing short of spiritual genius).[8] And saints play an important role in vigorously living out the ideals of their religious tradition, showing new ways of presenting its religious vision and giving a prophetic judgement on its inadequate embodiments.[9] But why should they

sometimes cause a religious conversion? One reason might be
that saints seem, as Richard Swinburne puts it, to have 'got the
measure of life', so that we ought to trust their beliefs.[10] But I think
that my quotation from de Lubac suggests a much stronger
reason: God is sensed through the saints, for they are believed to
be like God, and not only this, but made like Him because God is
believed to be *in* them, moulding them to His image. Hence
Tolstoy said of his contemporary the *staretz* Amvrosy 'when one
talks with such a man, one feels the nearness of God'.[11] Of course,
all creation reflects God's glory; but the saints are believed to tell
us of His personal qualities, especially His Love. It is almost as if
God smiled on the world from behind their eyes. The saints are
believed, too, to tell us something of His power, for in them our
weak human nature has been shaped into something strong and
fine. Hence in the essay from which I quoted in Chapter 1 Karl
Rahner draws attention to the importance of the saints in showing
that the church is not merely for sinners, for those *in via*, but is
also the church of victorious grace and eschatological salvation:

> God really *has* redeemed, he really *has* poured out his Spirit, he
> really *has* done mighty things for sinners, he *has* let his light
> shine in the darkness . . . she [the Church] must not declare this
> merely as a *possibility* provided by God . . . as if one could merely
> 'presume' that God has poured out his Spirit without giving any
> evidence at all of his mighty wind and his tongues of fire.[12]

PHILOSOPHY AND THE SAINTS

There is a flavour of apologetics in this passage. There are also
some philosophical assumptions latent here and in some of the
other passages I have discussed. It is assumed that certain
phenomena in the world are *effects* brought about by the spirit of
God, and that such effects resemble their cause: St Paul speaks of
men being changed by degrees into the likeness of God by the
Spirit (II Cor. iii, 18), and Aquinas maintains that human perfections like goodness and wisdom are caused by, and participate in,
their divine exemplars (*S.T.* 1a xiii. 5, 6, 10; xiv.6). To parody Scripture, by *their* fruits you shall know *Him*. Because of this, it is
assumed too that sanctification may be regarded as *evidence* of

God's nature and activity, and indeed, this is explicitly stated by Newman:

> As 'the heavens declare the glory of God' as Creator, so are the saints the proper and true evidence of the God of Christianity, and tell out into all lands the power and grace of Him who made them . . . They are the popular evidence of Christianity.[13]

More recently, Professor H. H. Price has drawn the phenomenon into the ambit of Natural Theology, using it as experimental evidence for God's existence.[14]

Such assumptions about sanctification have not been discussed much by philosophers, at least in recent times. Yet this is surprising, for the phenomenon of human transformation raises many interesting philosophical questions: about its moral value, about its nature and causes, and – as a consequence of this – about the way it is to be described.

Most obviously it raises questions about ethics, for words like 'saintly' are evaluative: they are what Professor R. M. Hare calls 'supervenient' terms, dependent on the ascription of a range of other qualities. But which qualities? I have talked rather blithely about transformation and sanctification, but the fact remains that there are different kinds of human transformation and different models of sanctity. It is a disturbing experience to read of some saint and to find him or her morally repellent in certain respects. In her very interesting correspondence with a journalist Antonia White records this feeling. She says:

> But, when I read, as I read today of St. Catherine of Siena, that in crushing her natural affections, she turned away from her mother's caresses 'with as much abhorrence as if they had been poison', I am deeply and instinctively revolted . . . this element seems to be in all the saints who are held up to us as ideals, and it seems to me morbid and perverse.[15]

This feeling may be aroused by a whole pattern of life as well as by particular individuals. The most obvious examples are Nietzsche's attack on Christian morality, and Luther's comment on monasticism: 'However numerous, sacred, and arduous they may be, these works, in God's sight, are in no way whatever superior to the works of a farmer labouring in the field, or of a woman

looking after her home'.[16] More recently we have seen a deprecia-
tion of asceticism and also the development of what one might
call the 'spirituality of secularism': the insistence that Christians
should not be detached from the world but should participate in
social movements and even revolutionary politics. Perhaps the
pendulum has swung back a bit during the last few years, since I
detect an awakening interest in traditional spirituality, prayer and
contemplation. But even here the interest is often motivated by a
feeling that real service in the world requires a developed life of
prayer as its basis.

As far as Christianity is concerned I do not think it is necessary
to insist on a single pattern of sanctity, for it has always been
recognised that there are different patterns of saintliness and
spirituality; compare for instance, St Jerome and St Francis of
Assisi, St Bernard and St Francis of Sales, John Wesley and Dr
Johnson, Dietrich Bonhoeffer and Dorothy Day. Still, I think that
we must ask ourselves two questions here: are there some
characteristics which we must exclude in every case, for instance
gross lack of charity? and are there some which are always
necessary (like the note of joy in the life and influence of a saint)?
Certainly, too, St Paul's list of the fruit of the Spirit is very specific
about the characteristics which are necessary: love, gentleness,
patience, kindness and so on.

It seems, therefore, that religious people may be called upon to
justify their moral criteria of sanctity. In practice, of course, they
are not usually much worried by ethical relativism: disputes are
nearly always about specific problems, for example the morality of
warfare, divorce or abortion. And although Christians and Jews
may attempt to defend their moral views in general by appealing
to philosophical considerations and to the teachings of the Law,
the prophets or Christ, in the case of sanctity the holiness of God is
regarded as the exemplar. If men must be holy because God is
holy and He sanctifies them, then the *imitatio Dei* is the road to
holiness for men. Now God is described as compassionate,
gracious, long-suffering, ever constant and true, forgiving,
securing justice for widows and orphans, and loving the alien
living among the Jews (Ex. xxxiv.6; Dt. x.17f); hence the Jew must
'walk in the ways of God' by modelling his conduct on God's
actions, particularly by showing mercy, patience and forbearance
(Dt. x.19, xiii.5; Is. lviii.2; lxi.8; Jer. ix.23; xxii.16; Ps lxviii.6). This
message is repeated by Christianity ('Be merciful, even as your

Father is merciful' – Lk. vi.36; cf. Mt. v.48), but now there is also
believed to be a mediator between God and man, Jesus Christ.
Hence it refers more to the imitation of Christ, than of God
(though, as we have seen, it describes Christ as the image of the
Father).

Despite this common background, there are a few ethical
differences between Judaism and Christianity. For instance,
asceticism plays a much smaller role in the former than the latter:
G. F. Moore quotes a rabbinical saying: 'A man will have to give
account on the judgement-day of every good thing which he
might have enjoyed and did not'.[17] The position becomes more
difficult when we consider religions other than Christianity. The
clash between religions is not always a matter of conflicting
doctrines: it is often a moral conflict, about the value of detach-
ment and asceticism, about the value of different possibilities of
spiritual renewal, about what constitutes sin or salvation (and of
course some religions have *no* concepts of sin and salvation). Such
conflicts gain added depth from psychological factors, when
commitment to spiritual ideals is motivated by devotion to a
particular historical person. In theistic religions the moral
considerations which I have mentioned are also important
because of the belief already mentioned, that certain worldly
perfections, like love, mercy and justice, are to be taken as reflections of God's characteristics (hence these ethical problems are
connected with the ontological issues which I shall discuss next).
This belief assumes that we know what constitutes a perfection
and whether God has it (for presumably we must rule out the
attribution of qualities like thankfulness, courage or chastity to
God).[18] Perhaps this shows that one cannot do theology until one
has got one's ethics straight! Certainly it needs to be noted that
people's moral views have always tended to influence their
theology: the Greek philosopher Xenophanes complained that
'Homer and Hesiod have attributed to the gods everything that is
a shame and reproach amongst men, stealing and committing
adultery and deceiving each other' (Kirk and Raven, *Frag.* 169).
This complaint was repeated by Plato and used by him as the basis
for a proposal for censoring religious myths (*Republic* 377E–391E)
– an early example of using moral considerations to recast
theology. As a more recent example one could mention the way
in which John Stuart Mill's moral views led him to attack predestination, everlasting punishment, substitutionary punishment

and retributive justice as bad moral doctrine; he was one of many who have found it hard to reconcile modern views about penal reform with the doctrine of Hell (though it could be claimed that it is precisely Christian teaching about pity, mercy and love which has led to change of views about both human and divine punishment). In general, it seems that when people cease to find a conception of God admirable, they end up finding it incredible.[19]

Such ethical differences are not beyond discussion, any more than others are. But any defence of religious positions on ethical matters usually requires that one takes a wide view, and sees how the moral principles of a religion relate to its other teachings and practices. An adequate understanding of Christian asceticism, for example, would require a consideration of the ideas of sacrifice, renunciation and atonement in general, and particularly of Christ's self-renunciation in the Incarnation (*kenōsis*), his suffering and death on the Cross; and a differentiation of Christian from Manichaean views of the world.

Let us assume, however – what is not impossible – that we have managed to reach some agreement on ethical questions and that we have a certain set of virtues which we regard as wholly admirable.[20] Let us assume, too, that we find a set of people who embody these virtues to a high degree, who have not always done so, and who have been helped to do so through the practice of a religion. In other words, they have been transformed into saintly people. What does this show?

The first question which suggests itself is: what has caused the change? Now any outer transformation visible to others is likely to be accompanied by an inner life of a distinctive kind. This will, of course, include prayer, meditation and other religious practices. It may also include religious experiences (though this is not necessarily so). Many saints have been converted or deeply influenced by religious experiences of different kinds: St Paul, St Francis of Assisi and St Ignatius Loyola, for example. Others have continued to have such experiences, sometimes of a fairly exotic kind, as with St John of the Cross, sometimes of a humbler kind, as with Brother Lawrence and his sense of the presence of God. But many religious writers have warned against the tendency to put too much stress on such experiences, for they are not a necessary part of saintliness. Thomas Merton, for instance, writes:

> We must remember that our experience of union with God, our feeling of His presence, is altogether accidental and

secondary. It is only a side effect of His actual presence in our souls, and gives no sure indication of that presence in any case ... Do not desire chiefly to be cherished and consoled by God; desire above all to love Him.[21]

What is more important than any episodic religious experience is the continued ordering of the inner life, not just in prayer and so on, but also in the development of attention and recollection and (something ignored in much traditional spiritual writing) in the education of the emotions. Many philosophers in recent decades have attacked the popular view that emotions are simply blind forces which arise in our minds, and which cannot be trained or ordered. Sartre, for instance, brings out their 'intentional 'quality, by which he means the way in which we are conscious of and respond to the world:

> Emotion is not an accident, it is a mode of our conscious existence, one of the ways in which consciousness understands (in Heidegger's sense of *Verstehen*) its Being-in-the-World. A reflective consciousness can always direct its attention upon emotion.[22]

Now if they are not to be regarded as experiences we have or as urges which just come over us, but are closely related to our beliefs, values and the way we live, then we have a greater degree of responsibility for our emotions and desires than is usually realised. Here is an area where greater self-knowledge may lead to greater self-control. This can, of course, be merely a narcissistic exercise in self-cultivation. But for the religious person real self-knowledge requires the illumination of the Holy Spirit; and anyway it is only a means to an end, that of having God dwell in us, change us and shine out from us. The ultimate goal of recollectedness is purity of heart, whereby we will and do what is good naturally and spontaneously. Thus Fr Yelchaninov says:

> It is not behaviour, words and actions which are essential, but what fills our heart. The good deed is not the one which appears good, but which springs forth from the fullness of the merciful heart; it is the same with wicked words and deeds which are but the off-shoot of a heart full of evil forces. To be good is not to be trained to do good actions, but to accumulate

the warmth of grace in one's heart, above all through purification and prayer. In order not to suffer from the frost, we must be inwardly warm.[23]

Recent philosophers have also stressed the close relationship between the inner and outer aspects of man (this stress has often gone hand in hand with a rejection of Dualism, but this is not necessarily the case). They do not deny that there is a realm of inner, private experience (how could they?), but they emphasise that the inner and outer are closely connected, that they are two aspects of one entity, the person, and that much of our language about human beings describes both aspects. Thus Wittgenstein, for example, argues that terms like 'understanding' and 'intending', do not merely denote inner private processes, for it is the circumstances in which these occur and the accompanying or ensuing behaviour that are also part of this meaning. The relevance of this line of thought to a consideration of spirituality is plain: it is not something to do merely with the private realm of inner experience, for we are concerned with the whole man, with total self-transformation. Again, this is not to deny that there is an inner life of prayer and reflection, but the point is that this should bear fruit in external behaviour. 'If things are going badly in the inner life, it will become clear externally.'[24] The connection is not merely a psychological, causal one; for there is also a logical one, which holds in virtue of the fact that there are some behavioural criteria for the ascription of terms like 'grace', 'faith' and 'conversion'. Hence they do not denote only inner states, processes and experiences. An inner process would not *count* as 'conversion', for example, unless there was some way, at least in principle, in which it could be manifested.[25]

So far I have been speaking mainly about the causes of sanctification that are within a man, in the sense of being linked to the private life of prayer and devotion. But there are also 'external' causes to be considered. Some of these are uncontroversial: the example of a paradigmatic figure, the influence and encouragement of friends, colleagues or religious superiors, and the support of a religious community. But religious people often appeal to a cause that is external in another sense, namely the spirit of God, and such an appeal obviously raises philosophical problems. Of course, they are not denying that there are certain capacities involved, that there is a 'learning how', and that the factors just mentioned play a part. They are, however, also appealing to the slow work of God's spirit, gradually healing and transforming. Now why do we need such a 'supernatural' explanation of saint-liness? Isn't it enough to appeal to the other factors? Isn't it illegitimate to hypostatise an 'influence' or a 'power', and to treat the 'spirit' which one person can transmit to another as having an independent existence?

These objections bring us back to some of the questions raised at the end of the last chapter. Clearly the main consideration for religious believers is that sanctity is not regarded as being achieved by one's own efforts, something of which one could be proud: 'it is no longer I who live, but Christ who lives in me' (Gal. ii.20). This is not just undue humility, for they appeal sometimes to particular religious experiences and, more often, to the notion of a spiritual power, a power which is 'outside' them in the sense of being independent of them, and which changes them. There are some things which one cannot produce oneself, and for which one should not take credit; one can only wait patiently. Things like a religious discipline and the example of others are contributing factors, but they do not inevitably produce the same desired results. Heroic virtue is a rare thing, not to be expected in the ordinary course of events.

Yes, but may not the hidden factor which the religious believer describes as grace or as the Holy Spirit really be something from within us? May it not be an irruption from the subconscious? The obvious answer to such objections is that *of course* it is within us! For how could God achieve our spiritual renewal except by working through us? The idea that the relevant factors may be irruptions from the unconscious was already made by William James: he suggests that they are such on the 'hither' side, and that on the 'further' side there is God's power.[26] Again, the idea of secondary causality is important here: there is no reason why the spirit of God should not work through 'natural' means, in this case the powers of our mind.[27]

It is unlikely that one will reach agreement on this question simply by arguing along the lines I have indicated. Usually those who proffer 'naturalistic' explanations of sanctity already have a bias towards such explanations in general; and those who appeal to the Holy Spirit do not do so merely because they cannot find any naturalistic explanation, for if this were so they would be reducing the matter to crude apologetics, making the Holy Spirit a 'god of the gaps', and forgetting the role of secondary causes. The latter use terms like 'grace', 'Holy Spirit', 'redemption', 'salvation' and so on because they are trying to put sanctity in its context, in a religious tradition, and to connect it with other factors in that tradition. These terms are analogous to the 'theory-laden' terms of science, in that a phenomenon visible to all is brought within a wider picture of description and explanation.

RELIGIOUS AND SCIENTIFIC EXPLANATIONS

It will be worth taking this point further, for there is some analogy between theological systems and scientific theories, besides the fact that they use a special theory-laden terminology. In the case of the latter a number of facts are covered by an explanation, which may appeal to theoretical constructs like 'electrons' and may involve the use of a model. The relationship between the facts about the world and the explanation is complex, and it is not always possible to devise a crucial experiment to test the explanation. Similarly, a developed historical religion like Christianity is concerned with various kinds of putative facts and it uses different levels of description. In particular, Christians appeal to events in the past, the present and the future, and seek to link all three: they appeal to historical facts about Jesus Christ, to the present life in the world (which is where the question of sanctification comes in), and to the future life after death. They believe that the kind of life they lead today will affect their fate after death, and that both of these in turn are affected by the redemptive work of Christ. Moreover, above all three there is, as it were, the overarching fact of God's presence and activity. Hence all three spans of time are described in theistic categories: the past in terms of God's incarnation in Christ, the present in terms of Providence, grace, holiness and the presence of the Holy Spirit, and the future in terms of divine forgiveness, salvation and more specifically eschatological categories. Some religious concepts seek to connect the different stages. Thus the term 'redemption' uses a legal analogy to link several kinds of fact: Jesus Christ's work and death, men's past sins and present spiritual progress, the life to come, and (throughout all) God's grace and forgiveness.

It is the present span of time with which I am now concerned, and particularly with the existence of saintly people. What has happened is this: the transformation of man into saintliness is often so impressive and attractive that it is felt to require an explanation; people wish to discern the conditions of the 'new life', to give some account of the nature of the spiritual forces which take possession of individuals (and sometimes communities). If explanations in terms of psychology and education seem inappropriate or insufficient, for the reasons already suggested, and if the transformation has occurred in the practice of a religion, then a religious explanation may be sought, typically in terms of some kind of 'power' or 'spirit'. The religious explanation is analogous to a scientific one in that it relates the phenomenon under consideration to other facts and seeks to assign a cause. To be more specific, the religious believer links present sanctity with past history and the future life, seeing it as the effect of one and as a determinant of the other; and he also links it with the presence of God over all: the saints are *signs* of God's continuing activity and of His future kingdom.

Because it is drawn into this explanatory scheme, the phenomenon is described in a special 'theory-laden' terminology. Even simple terms like 'holy' and 'sanctity' were originally religious, though they have now lost much of their earlier flavour. A term like 'grace' is more obviously 'loaded': it seeks to link the present spiritual strength and goodness of men with the love of God and the redemptive work of Christ. In Eastern Orthodox theology it is often linked with the concept of *theōsis*: grace is regarded as the 'divinising energies' which the Holy Spirit communicates to man, thereby penetrating and transforming his whole being, and giving a foretaste of the Kingdom of God.

Since these terms are interlocked with a whole theological system we cannot simply point to the saints and say 'That is what I mean by "grace" ' or 'That is supernatural'.[28] Of course, we have to teach people the meaning of the terms, and pointing to the saints is one way of starting (in particular, I think that this is a good starting-point for a consideration of the doctrine of the Holy Spirit). Many religious concepts *do* involve reference to spiritual transformation, and many religious doctrines attempt to describe and explain the possibilities of acquiring such a transformation. But this is only part of their function, for the use of terms like 'grace' and 'Holy Spirit' indicate that facts about human life and history are being interpreted in terms of something beyond them, a power operating at different times and places and not part of our own resources.

A non-believer may well recognise and admire the phenomenon of sanctity, but he will reject its religious interpretation. He does not regard human transformation as being caused by God's grace and as reflecting His qualities. This explains why he may reject also the very language in which it is described by religious people. It is felt that this language brings with it a lot of metaphysical baggage, as it were. A startling example of this feeling is to be found in Kant's *Religion within the Bounds of Reason Alone*. There he discusses the use of the term 'grace': he admits that certain inexplicable movements leading to a great moral improvement do occur in people, but he insists that we cannot distinguish between the effects of nature and grace, because we cannot recognise a supra-sensible object within our experience; hence he labels 'grace' as a 'transcendent idea'.[29]

I think Kant is over-stating his point, since a man may feel the 'givenness' of grace without necessarily wishing to claim any acquaintance with the giver: believers have usually said that God is beyond their direct experience and full comprehension. Moreover, he does not do full justice to the concept of a spiritual power: to the feeling which some people have that they are being changed by a power outside them, against their own natures and even against their wills (a 'strength not our own', as von Hügel puts it[30]). But Kant is certainly right in pointing to the fact that theistic religions do tend to move easily from the spiritual to the ontological, and that this move involves going from our experience to what is beyond our experience.

Of course, we might answer Kant by returning to my parallel between religious systems and scientific theories. Appeal to entities beyond our experience is permissible in the latter (a development not foreseen by Kant, and perhaps not really catered for in his philosophy), so possibly it may be so in the former. It needs to be noted, however, that the parallel is only partial. The analogy lies in three factors: use of special 'theory-laden' language, appeal to unseen entities, and the explanatory role of these entities. But the parallel breaks down in at least three important ways:

(1) The entities appealed to in theology, for example the Holy Spirit, are personal, and thus the relevant kind of explanation is so, that is it appeals to personal concepts like 'love',

'desire' and 'fidelity', and it takes account of human freedom.
(2) Similarly, these entities are not part of the spatio-temporal
    world, in the way that the theoretical constructs of science
    are. They are immaterial and in some sense transcendent. It
    would seem silly to expect that future research will
    assimilate the Holy Spirit to a bacterium, as Grover Maxwell
    hopes that electrons will be.[31]
(3) As a consequence, the entities appealed to in theology are
    unobservable, and therefore outside the range of scientific
    experiment and prediction. Kai Nielsen, as we saw in the
    last chapter, argues that we could never identify incorporeal
    agents or spirits, and that it is improper to ascribe personal
    attributes to them. But, more specifically, he objects to the
    parallel sometimes made between theoretical entities like
    mesons or protons and religious beings, because it is
    logically impossible to observe the latter: it would be
    contradictory to say 'They have finally observed God'.[32]
    Moreover, we cannot employ religious terms in theories
    which we then use to make predictions to be verified or
    falsified.[33]

These three points do not, however, entail that we must com-
pletely reject the parallel. As regards the first one, the personal
nature of religious entities does not mean that we must rule out all
prediction here, although experimental testing is ruled out as
inappropriate. For, although 'the wind [or spirit] blows where it
wills' (Jn iii.8), a personal agent believed to have attributes like
goodness, love, mercy and fidelity cannot be entirely unpredict-
able: for example, if God is indeed faithful, then presumably He
must keep His promises (if these can be identified!) and answer
those who serve Him. Likewise, although God is transcendent in
the sense that He exists apart from the world and could exist
without it, He is also believed to be present and active in the
world; so presumably *qua* an agent immanent in the world He *is*
spatio-temporal. Here, again, my analysis of the concept of a spirit
is important, in showing us one form of divine activity, that of
spiritual power.
   The concept of a spiritual power and its effects also has implications for the third question, that of verification and falsification. I
think that it would be a mistake to use the occurrence of saintliness as the premise of an argument to prove God's existence. For

the existence of a causal link between sanctification and God's action does not necessarily mean that we can now construct a direct argument from one to the other: even if it is agreed that there is a source of sanctity and that this source is personal, it remains to be shown that it is God or the Holy Spirit rather than, say, Apollo, and that the God who heals and nourishes the soul also created the world; and even if we believe that there is a creator we require an argument for monotheism, showing that the creator is also the sanctifier. Fortunately, however, there are other logical and epistemological relations which we can consider. It is possible that the occurrence of sanctification *is evidence for* the existence of God: for if the occurrence requires explanation, the activity of God is one possible explanation; moreover, looking at it another way, the occurrence is something to be expected, given belief in the Judaeo-Christian God, and therefore it confirms this belief (assuming that we have other grounds for it).[34] This relationship is a weaker one than logical entailment, for it allows that there could be other explanations of the occurrence to be explained.

The evidential relationship is connected with that of falsification, in that lack of relevant evidence tends to falsify a hypothesis. My analogy between religious conceptual schemes and scientific ones suggests, in any case, that we ought to look at the relationship of falsification. Its relevance is this: I have drawn attention to the wide-ranging nature of religious systems like Christianity, and the way in which they link together claims of different kinds. Some of these are truth-claims concerned with the present, and specifically with the possibility of sanctification through the indwelling of God's spirit. Now if Christians were never changed by the practice of their religion, this would count against, if not decisively refute, certain important Christian doctrines: in particular, it would tell against those of grace and of the sending of the Holy Spirit, and thereby call into question our view of divine activity. Hence a failure to continue to produce saints would count against the truth of Christianity, because certain of its crucial doctrines require that men be changed by God. The common objection to Christianity that Christians are not better than they are (as Nietzsche said, 'they don't look redeemed') can be regarded as an implicit appeal to falsification. It would, of course, be very difficult to tell empirically that there were no saints or that Christians were not improved by the practice of their religion.

That is one reason why I have used the weaker terminology of 'tell against' and 'count against', rather than the stronger 'refute' or 'disprove', although texts like Isaiah lix.21, John xiv. 16 (the promises that God's spirit or the Counsellor will be given forever) and Gal. v.22f (the list of the fruit of the Spirit) suggest that the stronger language might be warranted. It would be difficult to quantify the presence of virtues to the degree that seems necessary for an absolute falsification argument. Nevertheless, the logical relationship remains.

CONCLUSION

My own final position, then, involves two claims:

(1) Religious believers point to something that is to some extent visible and recognisable to everyone, saintliness (even if not all admire it), but they use special terms to describe it, because they have a special ontological model of the world in which the present sanctification of man is linked to facts of other kinds. The phenomenon of sanctity is thus drawn into a wide-ranging conceptual scheme, which is analogous to a scientific theory in *some* respects.

(2) The existence of saintly people is a truth-condition of Christianity and many other theistic religions, in that the absence of saints would tend to falsify some doctrines. I do not think that the existence of saints verifies theism in the strong sense of conclusively establishing its truth; but it *is evidence for* its truth – a weaker relationship – for the existence of saintliness is something which requires an explanation, and theism provides one such explanation, in terms of the presence of God's spirit.

One of the advantages of appealing to falsification rather than verification is that the existence of saintly people who are unbelievers or members of non-theistic religions is not a difficulty. It is only a problem if you are using the existence of saints to prove the truth of your own religion; for then the existence of saints in other religions, the beliefs of which are incompatible with your own, may raise a difficulty analogous to that raised by Hume concerning the apologetical value of miracles. Of course, in practice Christians have often tended to brush aside non-Christian saintliness as merely due to natural virtue or even of little account ('the glittering vices of the pagans', to use St Augustine's phrase). But recently some theologians have questioned such *a priori* dogmatism about the outreach of God's grace, for it attempts without sufficient justification to set limits to God's mercy and love, as well as seeming to fly in the face of the facts.[35] We find a similar liberality in some of the early Christian Fathers: St Leo the Great for instance, says:

> When on the Day of Pentecost the Holy Spirit filled the disciples of the Lord, it was not so much the beginning of a gift as it was the completion of one already bountifully possessed: because the patriarchs, the prophets, the priests, and all the holy men who preceded them were already quickened by the life of the same Spirit . . . although they did not possess his gifts to the same degree.[36]

If one adopts a more generous view of the workings of divine grace, then it is only the *absence* of saints in a theistic religion which raises a real difficulty, since such an absence tends to falsify theism. As regards saintly people outside Christianity, they may well, if they show forth qualities akin to the fruit of the Holy Spirit, be subjects of God's grace (even though they may lack this concept). Thus the Buddhist *arhat*, who has a mind and heart free from craving and is at peace, ready for *nirvána*, may be receiving divine grace.[37]

I am aware that, despite this and other advantages, my second claim is likely to seem far more controversial than my first, and I put it forward more tentatively. Certainly it has always been true that Christianity has produced saintly people, and I take this to be a sign of God's fidelity to His promises. Yet it is conceivable that this should no longer be the case, for a time or even for good. Various theological responses would be possible in such a hypothetical situation. One is that sanctification is only achieved eschatologically, and that in this world righteousness is imputed to the justified. But this is hard to reconcile with belief that the Holy Spirit is present now. No doubt full perfection is realised only in Heaven, but in the saints we have examples of people who achieved an outstanding degree of goodness in this life. Moreover, surely there is a link between justification and righteousness?

Although Luther denied that justification can be earned through good works, nevertheless he insisted that it must, if genuine, be manifested in them:

> Faith, however, is something God effects in us. It . . . makes us quite different men in heart, in mind, and in all our powers; and it is accompanied by the Holy Spirit . . . it is impossible indeed, to separate works from faith, just as it is impossible to separate heat and light from fire.[38]

Another response might be that the number of the Elect is full and that the work of the Holy Spirit is accomplished. But this suggestion would depend on a particular view of predestination and would set temporal limits to the work of the Holy Spirit. A more complex response might be that people had become so evil that they resisted God's grace: after all, sainthood has to be prepared for, it is not just a phenomenon which happens. It is therefore conceivable that a situation might arise in which because no one was prepared for sanctity, the grace was not bestowed: the Holy Spirit was indeed still present, but was unrecognised or rejected, and grace was available but not taken up.

The third response raises interesting but difficult problems in the theology of grace. I am inclined to think that it contains an excessively Pelagian view of grace, suggesting that it can be earned. Surely the 'preparation' needed for sanctity is itself a co-operation with grace that has been given? Moreover, what would the power of the Holy Spirit and of grace amount to in a situation in which *all* men rejected them? What would we make of Christ's promise that the Holy Spirit is given for ever? My theological difficulties with this and the other two responses outlined lead me to reaffirm my initial position: that the situation envisaged in which there were no longer any saints, would indeed count against certain important Christian doctrines. But the variety of possible responses shows something of the complexity of theology, and points up both the analogies and the differences between scientific theories and theological explanations.

4   First Fruits

At the beginning of this book I quoted some examples of the claim that the presence of the spirit of God, seen most clearly in saintly people, is an anticipation of the life to come. Some of the writers quoted, for instance Wesley, were careful to say that an 'anticipation' is something more than a 'preparation', for it is believed that the life of the Blessed has already begun on this earth. In a similar vein, von Hügel concludes his encyclopaedic study *Eternal Life* by saying:

> Religion, in its fullest development, essentially requires, not only this our little span of earthly years, but a life beyond. Neither an Eternal Life that is already fully achieved here below, nor an Eternal Life to be begun and known solely in the beyond, satisfies these requirements. But only an Eternal Life already begun and truly known in part here, though fully to be achieved, and completely to be understood hereafter, corresponds to the deepest longings of man's spirit as touched by the prevenient spirit, God. (p.396)

The claim that the life to come is already present to some degree now is an example of what has come to be known as 'inaugurated' or 'partially realized' eschatology (to adapt C. H. Dodd's phrase).

Now that we have studied the concepts of a spirit and of saintliness, it is time to move on to consider the connection between them and immortality. There are many passages in Scripture which can be quoted as pointing to such a connection. St Paul often links the Holy Spirit with the Christian's hope (e.g. in Rom. xv.13, Gal. v.5). But, more specifically, he speaks of those who sow to the Spirit reaping eternal life from it (Gal. vi.8), of sanctification having eternal life as its end (Rom. vi.22f), and he says:

> If the Spirit of him who raised Jesus from the dead dwells in you, he who raised Christ Jesus from the dead will give life to

51

your mortal bodies also through his Spirit which dwells in you. (Rom. viii.11)[1]

He uses the metaphors of 'first fruits' and 'earnest':[2] the Spirit is the first fruits of our adoption as sons and of the redemption of our bodies (Rom. viii.23), an earnest of our heavenly dwelling and of the swallowing up of what is mortal by life (II Cor. v.5; cf. i.22); and the seal of the Holy Spirit is the earnest of our inheritance (Eph. i.13f; cf. iv.30). Similarly, the Epistle to the Hebrews uses the metaphor of a 'foretaste', speaking of those who 'have become partakers of the Holy Spirit, and have tasted the goodness of the word of God and the powers of the age to come . . .' (vi.4f). The Fourth Gospel often speaks of eternal life as being a present possession (e.g. in iii.36), but on three occasions such passages are immediately followed by references to our being raised at the last day (v.24–9, vi.40, 54), perhaps suggesting that one is an anticipation of the other.

A variation on this theme is the claim that it is the Holy Spirit who will raise men from the dead. In Judaism the outpouring of God's spirit is associated with the final days. The Rabbinic teaching on Exodus xxxv.31 (where Bezalel is described as being filled with the spirit of God and endowed with skill, perception and knowledge) says 'In this world, my spirit hath given you wisdom, but in the time to come it will give you new life', citing Ezekiel, xxxvii.14, 'And I will put my spirit in you, and ye shall live'.[3] Christian writers are usually unwilling to say *simpliciter* that the Holy Spirit will raise us, presumably because this view would go against the claim that the Father raises the dead (Jn v.21). But St Paul, in Rom. viii.11 (already quoted), speaks of God giving life through His Spirit. Hence many Christian writers, both early and late, assign a central role to the Holy Spirit in our resurrection. St Basil, for instance, says that the Spirit causes both our renewal in this life and our resurrection from the dead (*On the Holy Spirit*, §49); and another early Christian writer, Niceta of Remesiana, quotes I Cor. xv.36 in his *Explanation of the Creed*, and then argues:

> I take it that He who raises to life the grain of wheat for the sake of man will be able to raise to life the man himself who has been sown in the earth. He both can and wills to do this. What the rains do for the seed, the dew of the Spirit does for the body that is to be raised to life.[4]

Barth gives the Holy Spirit a central role both in the raising of
Jesus and in our resurrection: he says that an important characteristic of the New Testament view of the resurrection of Jesus Christ
was that, as a free work demonstrating and revealing the grace of
the Father, it took place by the Holy Spirit;[5] and that the power of
the Holy Spirit will awaken us to eternal life (*C.D.* iv.iv. p.100).

THE STRUCTURE OF THE ARGUMENT

The claim at stake, then, is that the indwelling of the Holy Spirit,
which according to Gal. v.22f brings joy and peace as well as a
moral transformation, is not only a preparation for the future life
but an anticipation of it here and now. But what grounds are there
for thinking that this is so? What is the reason for thinking that the
present indwelling of the Spirit is indeed a prelude to something
greater?

One possible answer to my question is that the claim being
discussed is based not on arguments but on experience. In
ordinary life there are experiences, for example of great joy or
peace, when people became oblivious to the passage of time.
Josiah Royce argued that the experience of listening to music, in
which we are aware not only of the chord being played at a
particular moment but of the whole sequence of the piece, can
serve as an analogy of God's simultanaous awareness of all time.[6]
Similarly, it might be maintained that in religious experience,
particularly mysticism, people feel that they are 'transcending'
time and that they have a foretaste of the Beatific Vision.

I think that there is something of importance in this answer, but
that it cannot be the whole story. Louis Dupré is probably right
when he says that: 'The belief in life after death appears to have
grown out of actual experiences far more than out of reasoning
processes' (he instances experiences of transcendence).[7] But there
is a difference between a belief 'growing out of' some experiences
and it being grounded on them. People do indeed have 'timeless'
experiences. But what if death is after all the end, and such
experiences then cease? We need some reason for supposing that
they will indeed continue after death. I have already noted that
although the Fourth Gospel speaks of eternal life as a present
possession, it also indicates that those who possess it will be raised
at the last day.

A further point which requires to be made is that Wesley and others are not merely appealing to an experience, for they do not regard the indwelling of the Holy Spirit as such. There may be an experience of this indwelling, but it is not itself just an experience, any more than putting in a light-bulb is just an experience, although there is an experience of putting in a light-bulb. The essential thing about the indwelling of the Holy Spirit is that it is regarded as the source of new life and of moral transformation, of which the fruits should be visible to others.

So we are still left with the task of providing an argument to show that the indwelling of the Holy Spirit, seen particularly in the saints, is a 'first instalment' of the future life. But what kind of argument could this be? It does not seem to be the case that statements about the occurrence of saintliness entail statements about immortality, so a deductive connection is lacking. Nor have we found out by observation that some saints survive death, so that we can mount an inductive argument. So what alternative is there?

The answer, of course, is that there are more complex forms of argument. My contention will be that by adding further premises we can construct an argument maintaining that the occurrence of saintliness is evidence for immortality. These further premises are of a theological nature, so the argument is a theological rather than a philosophical one. Nevertheless, it is an argument with a clear logical structure and one which is, I believe, valid.

A clue to the nature of this argument is provided by C. H. Dodd, in his discussion of the concept of 'eternal life' in the Fourth Gospel. Referring to Jesus' linking of statements about the present possession of eternal life with those about the final resurrection, Dodd says: 'It is because the word of Christ has this power here and now that we can believe that it will have the same power hereafter'.[8] A similar argument is put forward by St Irenaeus, when, after quoting St Paul's remarks in II Cor. iii.3 about the Spirit writing on the tablets of the human heart, he says: 'If, therefore, in the present time, fleshly hearts are made partakers of the Spirit, what is astonishing if, in the resurrection, they receive that life which is granted by the Spirit?'[9]

It is, however, insufficient to appeal to the power of Christ or the Holy Spirit, since we need to know not only that they *can* grant immortality but that they *will* do so. Clearly the Christian will appeal here not only to God's power, but to His promises and His fidelity. And such an appeal is made by Irenaeus, though in a different context, in an earlier passage where he mentions the translation of Elijah and the preservation of Jonah and the men cast into the fiery furnace by Nebuchadnezzar, and sees these as demonstrating God's power, promise and fidelity, and therefore as confuting those who cannot believe that God can and will raise up their bodies to eternal life (*Adv. Haer.* v.v.2). Similarly, Barth points to the notion of promise that is implicit in St Paul's use of the terms 'first fruits', 'earnest' and 'seal' of the Spirit (*C.D.* iv.ii p.322).

What, then, is the logical structure of this argument? It can be put in the form of a *modus ponens* argument: if God can and will give the Holy Spirit (or eternal life) now, then He can and will raise men from the dead; but God has given, and continues to give, the Holy Spirit (or eternal life) now; therefore He can and will raise men from the dead. This formulation, however, does not advance matters very far, since the truth of the claim 'If God can and will give the Holy Spirit (or eternal life) now, He can and will raise men from the dead' is precisely what is at stake. What reason is there to think that dead men will be raised, and furthermore that they will be raised to the kind of fullness of life promised by Christianity (as compared, say, with the shadowy life endured by Achilles in Hades, as depicted in Homer's *Odyssey*)? The answer, I take it, is provided by the considerations raised in my last paragraph. God has promised both the gift of the Holy Spirit and immortality, and He has given and continues to give the former as an earnest. The giving of this earnest shows both God's power and his fidelity.

The argument which I have just adumbrated falls, I believe, into the hypothetico-deductive form of argument which is familiar in the sciences, though it is not exclusive to them. In this pattern of argument a hypothesis, suggested by certain evidence, is formulated and conclusions are deduced from it. In the case of the sciences these conclusions are then tested by further observation and experiment, and this fact differentiates the scientific and the religious cases;[10] but the logical form of the argument is the same. An example of such an argument in science is this:

Evidence: 100 parts (by volume) of oxygen combine with 200 parts of hydrogen to form water; 100 parts of muriatic gas combine with 100 parts of ammonia gas to form ammonia chloride . . .
Hypothesis: Gases combine in simple ratios by volume [Gay-

Lussac's law].
Deduction: The combination of gases F and G will be in simple ratios by volume.[11]
(If they do so combine, then we have further evidence for this hypothesis.)

Now the religious argument in question may be set out in a similar form:

> *Evidence*: God has given the Holy Spirit and continues to give it as He promised.
> *Hypothesis*: God is always faithful and effective.
> *Conclusion*: God will also give immortality, as He has promised.

There are, of course, many human analogies for such an argument, and St Paul's use of the term *arrabōn* (earnest) suggests the situation of a man fulfilling part of a contract as evidence of the trustworthiness. I think it is important for the theological argument that there *continue* to be saints manifesting the fruit of the Holy Spirit, for then evidence of God's power and fidelity is always visible. Lack of such evidence tends to falsify the hypothesis, for if God's promises have not been fulfilled, this is evidence against His power or His fidelity.

Clearly this argument, which I have maintained is a *theological* argument, depends on certain assumptions. It presupposes that the transformation seen particularly in the saints is an unexpected occurrence which is not to be explained simply in terms of natural causes, and that it is a manifestation of the Holy Spirit. It assumes that God has promised to bestow His spirit, and that He has kept His promise by bestowing it in the way described. Lastly, and most crucially, it assumes that we have a promise of immortality, and that one and the same being, God, has given this promise and the promise to send His spirit.

Clearly, too, the Christian religion defends these assumptions by appealing to the teaching of Jesus Christ: it was he, speaking on behalf of the Father, who promised both the Holy Spirit and immortality. Moreover, the Father confirmed his authority by raising him from the dead. These basic claims could be followed up by further appeals to God's fidelity and power, for example miracles. But it is important to see that the argument can be restated in ways other than those put forward by orthodox

Christians. Someone might accept Jesus' authority, without believing him to be God. Or people may accept some other authority,
for example a prophet, but put forward a similar argument: I take
it that Judaism does this, since it appeals to prophets like Ezekiel,
Joel and Daniel for its belief in immortality and the outpouring of
the Spirit of God (rather than the 'Holy Spirit' – though this term is
used on occasion in the Old Testament; cf. Ps li.11; Is. lxiii.10f).
Moreover, the argument may be boosted by other more general
considerations, for example by appeal to God's justice.

The sequence of the discussion so far can be summarised as
follows:

(1) *x* is an earnest of *y*.

Claims of this form raise two questions:

(2) What reason is there to think that *x* will continue at all?
(3) What reason is there to think that *x* will result in *y*?

A possible answer is:

(4) *A* has promised *x* and also its fulfilment, *y*, and has given
and continues to give *x* as an earnest.
(5) Thus we can construct a hypothetico-deductive argument,
using '*A* is always faithful and effective' as a hypothesis.

Further questions then arise:

(6) How do we know that one and the same being has
promised both *x* and *y*, and that this being is *A*?
(7) How do we know it is *A* that has given *x*?

A Christian would continue thus:

(8) *B* promised both *x* and *y*, on the authority of *A*.
(9) *A* raised *B* from the dead, and so confirmed his authority;
moreover, *A* showed thereby that he has the specific
power to raise men from the dead.
(10) Other arguments for the fidelity, power and justice of *A*.

The argument which I have outlined is only one among a number
of possible grounds for belief in immortality. Some people may

think it sufficient to believe in promises like 'I am the resurrection and the life; he who believes in me, though he die, yet shall he live' (Jn xi.25). But the argument, if valid, provides further grounds; and it explains the connection between holiness and immortality. It has certain similarities with other arguments for immortality. It is like Kant's argument in the *Critique of Practical Reason* in appealing to the notion of men's holiness: but it starts from holiness already (to some degree) achieved, rather than a demand of the practical reason which can only be fulfilled in an endless progress in an infinitely enduring existence (Bk.II, Ch.ii. §4). It is like some of the arguments used by the early Fathers in appealing to God's power and fidelity, such as Irenaeus' argument about certain Old Testament figures which I have already mentioned, or his later argument that the raising of Lazarus and others by Christ shows that his words concerning our future resurrection may also be believed (*Adv. Haer.* v.xiii.1). It is to be noted, too, that St Paul uses the same term 'first fruits' both of the Spirit which guarantees our redemption and of Christ's resurrection which anticipates that of others (Rom. viii.23; I Cor. xv.20, 23).

I have maintained that although the argument has a logical structure, it is a theological one which depends on certain assumptions. How, then, will it appear to those outside of the Judaeo-Christian tradition? The position with regard to a religious sceptic is fairly straightforward: clearly the argument will not convince him as an argument, since the assumptions involved in it are unlikely to be acceptable. But this does not mean that it is totally alien to him: after all, the example of people like Dietrich Bonhoeffer, Dag Hammarskjöld, Maximilian Kolbe and Mother Teresa of Calcutta in our own time may have a much greater influence in leading an unbeliever to give attention to the claims of religion than any theological argument. An unbeliever may greatly admire the characteristics which the believer calls the fruit of the Spirit, recognise that they are 'supernatural' in the weak sense of being unexpected and such as cannot be easily brought about simply by natural means, and so wonder how they are produced. He may even feel that saintly people are 'empowered' by something more than themselves, and wonder what this power is, and what are its characteristics. Clearly, however, these considerations stop a long way short of assent to any argument for immortality, though they perhaps indicate the beginnings of a road one might travel.

The position of other religions is more complicated. An easy way out is to say, again, that the argument is only applicable within Christianity, because it depends on certain assumptions (especially Christ's promises), and so it does not imply anything one way or the other about a future life for non-Christians. There are, however, one or two other considerations worth mentioning. I have indicated that an argument parallel in many respects to the Christian one is found in Judaism, so it would seem that in principle the argument could be extended to any theistic religion. Then, again, saintly people exhibiting characteristics similar to those called the fruit of the Spirit are found in other religions, even non-theistic ones (not to mention saintly unbelievers), and often they are regarded as having an eschatological significance, though the afterlife of which they are the 'first fruits' may be different from that envisaged by Judaism and Christianity. The Buddhist *arhat*, for example, is believed to have obtained release from the wheel of Reincarnation and to be ready for *nirvána*. The existence of such people is not a difficulty in itself, unless one assumes that only Christians may receive the Holy Spirit, and thereby gain salvation and immortality. There are a number of possibilities that can be suggested. Perhaps people achieving saint-liness in other religions may share the same fate as Christians; or perhaps they may come to the kind of future life that their own religions speak of — for why should not different forms of immortality or 'release' co-exist with each other? Or perhaps difficult eschatological teachings may be reconciled with each other: Geoffrey Parrinder has instanced the way in which belief in *nirvána*, first taught by Jains and Buddhists, apparently came into Hinduism through the *Bhagavad Gītā*, where it is seen as communion with God; the 'blowing out' indicated by the term is of desires and *karma*, not extinction of soul.[12] John Hick has attempted a reconciliation of all the eschatological and parescha-tological teachings of different major religions in his *Death and Eternal Life*.

THE LIFE OF THE AGE TO COME

It is not part of my argument to speculate about the nature of the future life. Nevertheless, there is one particular aspect of this question which needs to be pursued here, namely the likeness that is claimed between the life of a saintly person now and the life of the resurrection, since this seems to indicate something about the nature of the latter. The argument we are considering is not simply claiming that God has shown Himself faithful and effective in granting one thing He has promised, so He can be relied upon to bestow something further, for this would be to ignore the link between the two things promised. There is supposed to be an intrinsic connection between the two, in that one is not merely a preparation for the other, but also an anticipation of it. The healing and purification which is seen in the saints is regarded as part of a continuum.[13] This continuity is suggested by some of the metaphors which St Paul uses, especially 'first fruits' and 'earnest'. The latter is something more than a 'pledge' or 'guarantee', for the Greek term used, *arrabōn*, differs from the term *enechuron* (pledge) in that it denotes what is actually a small part of the whole that is promised, for instance, a portion of the purchase money given to ratify a contract.[14] Of course, one must be careful about inferring too much from the use of metaphors: and in the present context, we do not want to suggest that the future life will be merely 'more of the same'. In any case, the other analogies used, for example the seed in I Cor. xv.36ff and the tent and house in II Cor. v.1, suggest that there will be a great change within the continuity. A seed or a tent is not quite a 'first instalment' of a plant or a building.

Both common sense and philosophical considerations about the nature of identity suggest that there must be some likeness between the person on earth and the resurrected person, if they are indeed to be reckoned the same. But the specific question which we are considering is: why are the saints *more* like men of the age to come than ordinary people? There are a number of considerations to be taken into account here. The saints are believed to be already leading the best kind of life, being purified of sin and manifesting the fruit of the Holy Spirit. Moreover, in view of this they are growing in the likeness of God. Now since in the age to come those who have purified themselves will be like God (I Jn. iii.2f), it follows that there is also a likeness between them and the saints in this world (this assumes, of course, that the two sets of people are like God in the same respects). Thus Irenaeus says:

> But we do now receive a certain portion of His Spirit, tending towards perfection, and preparing us for incorruption . . . if the

earnest, gathering man into itself, does even now cause him to cry, 'Abba, Father', what shall the complete grace of the Spirit effect, which shall be given to men by God? It will render us like unto Him and accomplish the will of the Father; for it shall make man after the image and likeness of God. (*Adv. Haer.* v.viii.1, trans. Roberts and Rambaut)

If, then, there is a likeness between the saints now and the men of the age to come, it seems to follow that by looking at them we can know something about the future life. But there are a number of considerations which should warn us against trying to be too explicit about this. There is the risk of banality, which many putative descriptions of the after-life reveal.[15] Alternatively, imagination runs riot. Then there is a shift of context when the language of trust and hope (or of warning) is replaced by that of prediction. The prudent man, therefore, may well feel inclined to abandon any attempt to depict the state of the Blessed (or the damned), and instead content himself with indicating a few truth-conditions, largely negative (for example that consciousness does not cease forever at death). But even a minimal statement about what one's belief entails and excludes may raise several philosophical questions: for instance, the belief in the resurrection of the body raises questions about spatiality and location which have not received sufficient discussion.[16]

The argument about the connection between sanctity and immortality which I have discussed suggests, if it is valid, certain features of the future life: that it will have some continuity with our present life, that in it we shall be closer to God than we are on this earth, and that we shall be healed and made perfect. Will this life be a bodily life? The argument, I think, strongly suggests that it will be so, because the concept of saintliness seems to involve the concepts of activity and community, and they in turn suggest embodiment. Let us look at the list of the fruit of the Spirit given by St Paul in Gal. v.22f. Some of them could be possessed by a disembodied person: we can at least *imagine* what it would be like to be what Paul Helm calls a 'minimal person' who merely remembers, thinks, reasons and has dream-like perceptions,[17] and who in this state feels joy, peace and benevolence towards other beings. But how would such a 'minimal person' be able to act? Unless we can ascribe action and communication with others to such a being, then we cannot see what it would mean to describe it as gentle, patient and self-controlled, and as exercising love and kindness towards others. The same considerations apply, though to a less extent, to the dream-like existence envisaged by H. H. Price, in which people do have 'visual' images of their own bodies and interact with each other telepathically, but lack sense-perception and the power of acting through their limbs.[18] Hence it is difficult to see how there could be a communion of Saints, who manifest the fruit of the Spirit, without a bodily resurrection.[19]

If the life to come will be an embodied existence involving activity and community, this also suggests some considerations about another disputed question, whether this life will be in time, in the sense that change will continue. Some writers, for example Unamuno, have said that it must be, for man's highest aspirations are dynamic rather than static, and an eternity which was an eternal timeless present would allow no scope for creation or progression.[20] Others have envisaged a 'timeless' existence, of which philosophical contemplation or mystical experience give us some anticipation. But again, if the fruit of the Spirit will continue to be manifested in the age to come, this requires a dimension of time. Moreover, Kant's view of the acquisition of holiness as an endless progress likewise entails this. Hence his follower, Hermann Cohen, describes man's holiness as an 'infinite task', which 'consists in self-sanctification, which, however, can have no termination, therefore cannot be a permanent but only infinite striving and becoming'.[21]

These considerations, especially those concerning bodily exis-tence, are not, I think, decisive, since two considerations might be mentioned on the other side: the fruit of the Spirit listed by St Paul might be manifested only in this life,[22] and the saints in Heaven enjoy some other form of communion; and more seriously, since God (and possibly angels) can act and manifest goodness without possessing a body, then so can disembodied persons, even if we cannot now envisage how.[23] But, as it happens, both Judaism and Christianity do believe in a bodily resurrection, though on grounds other than that of the particular argument being dis-cussed (for example Christianity appeals to the bodily resurrection of Christ).

The Christian tradition, following St Paul, describes the bodies of those who have risen from the dead as 'spiritual' bodies. But this term is not, I think, to be taken as a description of the com-position of those bodies, as Origen supposed when he suggested that a spiritual body is one that is pure, refined and glorious, and therefore better suited to the purer etherial regions of heaven.[24] The term 'spiritual' (*pneumatikos*), is simply the adjective derived from *pneuma*, and St Paul uses it to denote a quality of relation-ship, not of substance.[25] The 'spiritual man' described in I Cor. ii.15 is no less corporeal than his 'unspiritual' *confrère* described in the previous verse, who is so because he does not receive the gifts of the Spirit of God and lacks spiritual discernment. Hence St Paul's contrast between a physical and a spiritual body in I Cor. xv.44 is not a statement about the substances of these bodies, but is to be explicated in terms of his contrast in the following five verses between the first Adam, the man of dust, and the last Adam, the man from heaven who became a life-giving spirit.[26] That this is the meaning of the term was realised by Irenaeus when, showing more discernment than Origen, he said that by 'spiritual' St Paul means partaking of the Spirit rather than lacking flesh; a being whose flesh was stripped away would be the spirit of a man (or of God), and not a spiritual man – who is a man possessing the earnest of the Holy Spirit and subject to the Spirit (*Adv. Haer.* v.vi.1, viii.2).[27] This is not to deny that there may well be striking differences between earthly bodies and resurrected bodies (St Paul says, for instance, that the latter are imperishable, in I Cor. xv.42), but the term 'spiritual' is not meant to describe what those differences will be. So, again, there seem to be good reasons for refraining from trying to be too explicit about the nature of the life to come. Moreover, since our discussion has dealt only with those people in whom the power of the Holy Spirit is discerned, it cannot tell us whether or not all will share in that life. But the argument we have been considering does commit us to saying that a saint is *more* like the men of the age to come than is an *homme moyen sensuel*.

5 Likeness To God

The idea of likeness to God plays an important role in the question discussed in the final section of the last chapter. But it has been implicit throughout the last three chapters: for it is believed that the Holy Spirit makes men like God, that the saints are more like God than ordinary men are, and that the men of the age to come will be like God. We find these beliefs expressed by some of the early Fathers of the church. Origen, for instance, says that 'The highest good is to become as far as possible like God' (De Princ. III.vi.1) and he distinguishes between God's image, which we received at our first creation and of which traces are manifest in our wisdom, justice, moderation, virtue and discipline (IV.iv.10), and the perfection of God's likeness. The latter 'was reserved for him [man] at the consummation. The purpose of this was that man should acquire it for himself, by his own earnest efforts to imitate God'.[1] The role of the Holy Spirit is spelt out by St Irenaeus, who describes him as the image of God (Adv. Haer. IV.vii.4) and says that the man made in the image and likeness of God is 'rendered spiritual and perfect because of the outpouring of the Spirit';[2] but, he says, in this life we receive only an earnest through the Holy Spirit, and the full image and likeness to God will be given only by the complete grace of the Holy Spirit (v.viii.1).[3]

Most people, when they hear the phrase 'likeness to God', will probably think of the statement in Genesis i.26 that man is created in the image and likeness of God, and perhaps also of the Christian idea that Christ is the very image of God and that men become more God-like by imitating Christ. But the concept of likeness to God is also found frequently in Greek philosophy. Plato, for instance, says in the Timaeus that the Creator 'was good . . . he desired that all things should be as like himself as they could be' (29E, trans. B. Jowett). More specifically, he tells us in the Theaetetus that men become like the divine, in so far as they can, by becoming righteous with the aid of wisdom, for in the divine there is no shadow of unrighteousness (176A ff).[4] Aristotle appeals to the concept in his discussion of the best kind of life for men in his *Nicomachean Ethics*, Bk. x. He influenced a long tradition in subsequent centuries through his conclusion that the contemplative life is the happiest and most god-like life (1178 B 8–23). Rather strangely, he fails to locate likeness to the gods in the moral life: he says that we cannot ascribe bravery and temperance to the gods for they cannot run risks, confront dangers or have bad appetites; likewise he rules out the ascription of justice and generosity to them, by construing these virtues in the narrow senses of making contracts, returning deposits and giving money or such things. Plato gives a much greater stress than Aristotle to the ethical aspect of the likeness, though of course for him ethics depends on intellectual factors (philosophical wisdom) and metaphysics (imitation of the Forms).

The Hebrew and the Greek traditions come together in Christian theology. The question of likeness to God was much discussed over the centuries, and gave rise to a lot of controversy at the Reformation and in modern times (notably between Barth and Brunner). It is a rich and fascinating area, both for philosophers and theologians, but it is beyond the scope of this chapter to discuss it fully.[5] I will have to rest content with addressing myself to the questions which are particularly relevant to my subject: why are the saints supposed to be more like God than other people are (this will require some discussion of the more general questions of which human attributes are God-like, and which of God's attributes can or should be imitated by men)? What is the role of the Holy Spirit in producing the likeness? And why do people desire such a likeness now and in the life to come?

FINDING WHERE THE LIKENESS HOLDS

The Bible stresses that there is a dissimilarity between men and God as well as a similarity. Although one can cull many texts which speak of a likeness between them,[6] there are contrary texts to be taken into account. Isaiah, in particular, emphasises God's difference: 'For as the heavens are higher than the earth, so are my ways higher than your ways and my thoughts than your thoughts . . . To whom will you liken me and make me equal, and compare me, that we may be alike?' (lv.9, xlvi.5; cf.xl.18). Some

Christian churches have stressed the unlikeness from the other direction, that of man, believing that the image of God bestowed in creation was lost at the Fall, or that only a remnant of it survived. But there is a more general religious reason for remind-ing people of the difference: religious worship seems to require an object that far surpasses any human quality – though this is not to say that it must be *totally* different (or 'wholly other'). If we stress only the likeness, we may tend to visualise God as, in Matthew Arnold's famous phrase, a kind of 'infinitely magnified and improved Lord Shaftesbury',[7] and thereby lose sight of His transcendence. We may also give the impression that God may be compared with creatures, so that one could say 'Like me, God is loving, faithful, intelligent ... ', a kind of remark which both sounds odd and savours of blasphemy.[8] But we can produce similar oddities without appealing to God:

> Like Einstein, I am intelligent
> Like Robert Redford, I am handsome

The anomaly is produced only by the suggestion of equality. But, of course, likeness is to be distinguished from sameness or equality, in having varying degrees. It might still, however, be argued that God is beyond any comparison: for how can an invisible and incorporeal being, God, be compared to a visible and corporeal one, man, especially when the former is said to be infinite, perfect and transcendent? The short answer to this objection is that people *do* compare the two, when they say things like

> God is wiser than any of us
> God is more loving than even our closest friends
> God will forgive when men will not
> God knows when I shall die, though I do not[9]

Moreover, it is commonly believed that even if God's perfections are indeed limitless, a good, holy and loving man is more like Him than is an evil one.

A fuller answer to the objection could require a thorough discussion of God's attributes. But we can go some of the way by considering His actions: as I remarked in a previous chapter, although God is believed to be transcendent, He is also believed to be immanent, to be an agent in this world. The Bible ascribes to Him actions like loving the stranger or securing justice for widows and orphans; and in my discussion of the concept of a spirit I tried to give some analysis of one mode of God's action, His penetration of men's hearts. So, if we can identify God's actions in this world, it would seem that we can compare His actions, and therefore His powers, with human ones, and consequently that we can compare God and man at least in some respects.

A more difficult question is to decide in what respects man can and should seek to become God-like. On both sides there are certain attributes which must be ruled out as applicable to both God and man. Certain of God's metaphysical attributes seem to be inapplicable to man, for example necessary being, omnipresence, eternity and possibly, though this is more controversial, immutability. Moreover, Rabbinic tradition excluded some other divine attributes, notably jealousy, vengeance, grandeur and circuity as properly applicable to men.[10] In some cases, the attributes cannot be shared by men, in others they should not be sought (for example vengeance), and in most cases they should not be sought because they cannot be attained (Aquinas remarks in *S.T.* 2a.2ae. clxiii.2 that Adam and Eve sinned by seeking an inordinate likeness to God through the knowledge of good and evil, whilst Lucifer sinned by craving to be like God in his might). On the other side, certain human qualities cannot be ascribed to God, not just evil qualities, but also some virtues, like Aristotle's examples of courage, temperance and chastity and Professor Geach's additional example of thankfulness.

How, then, do we go about composing our list of divine attributes which a person can achieve to some degree with the aid of God's grace, and which he or she should seek to attain? (I put that question in this way, in order to bypass disputes between Aquinas, Luther, Calvin, Barth, Brunner *et al.* about the state of Fallen man. Although they disagree about to what extent the image and likeness of God survived the Fall, they have a fair measure of agreement about what redeemed man should become, thanks to God's grace.) This question involves investigating both our sources of knowledge of the relevant attributes, and our principles of selection. There seem to be three possible approaches, which are not necessarily incompatible with each other.

First, picking a list of attributes from the Bible. Rabbinic tradition extracted thirteen characteristics of God as revealed in

His actions, as representing virtues for men to follow.[11] A Christian could carry out a similar task by studying the life of Christ.
This is an inductive approach and it does not by itself explain why
some attributes are comparable and others not.

Next, an *a priori* philosophical approach. Aquinas argues that all
perfections found in creatures exist pre-eminently in God; and
that anyway God is a self-subsistent being, so He must have every
conceivable perfection (*S.T.* 1a.iv.2); all perfections flow from Him
to creatures (*S.T.* 1a.xiii.5–6). This approach presupposes that we
know already what constitutes a perfection, and it argues deduc-
tively from certain assumptions; hence in principle it can clash
with the first approach (for instance, with regard to God's
immutability).

This approach also requires us to indicate some principles of
selection. We have already mentioned a few examples of attributes on either side which must be excluded, and hinted at some
principles of exclusion. Qualities specific to an infinite and
immaterial being cannot be applied to a corporeal one, for
example omnipresence. The converse is also true, hence again
courage, chastity and temperance cannot be ascribed to God (but
this is not to say that there is *nothing* in God which is remotely like
them: Rabbinic tradition regarded courage as akin to God's might
and 'heroism', alluding to Ex. xv.3 and Ps cvi.2, and Aquinas
regarded it as the mirror of the exemplar of God's unchange-
ableness).[12] God is also regarded as the Creator, and this gives him
certain prerogatives, particularly regarding the giving and taking
of life. Judaism restricts vengeance to Him, and also causing death
and reviving (that is resurrecting). It seems, then, that from 'above'
God's infinity and creativity and from 'below' man's finitude
(including his corporeality) and his sinfulness exclude certain
qualities as attributable to God or to be copied by man.

A third possible approach, one much less discussed than the two
just mentioned but particularly germane in view of our concerns
in this book, is through consideration of the Holy Spirit. It is
believed that God is known, particularly in His ethical attributes,
in the religious life. He is known through His worshippers: by this
I do not mean that we simply look at the focus of worship, for of
course this may just be a 'projection' of whatever human qualities
we admire, but that we look at the purification of man that is one
of the goals and fruits of religious practice. If this purification is
viewed as the slow action of the spirit of God, then it tells us not

only about the worshippers but also something about God's powers and actions. So here we *see* some of the latter as well as their effects on man: we see both because, as I argued in Chapter 2, a spirit is a particular kind of cause. It is a power which permeates the human heart, and which *indwells*.

THE SAINTS, CHRIST AND THE HOLY SPIRIT

All these three approaches explain why the saintly person is believed to be more like God than other people are: he or she is closer to God in many of His perfections,[13] whether these be known from Scripture, from *a priori* deduction or from discernment of His actions. I do not think that anything more needs to be said on this point.

There are, however, two important further considerations which Christianity introduces: firstly, in virtue of the fact that Christ is believed to be the perfect image of God, a middle term is introduced into the relationship of likeness between man and God. Christ is presented as telling us what God is like, and as the pattern for men to imitate. Secondly, more particular connections with the Holy Spirit are made.

The likeness of Christ is described in different ways. St Paul uses the term *eikón* (image): he tells us that Christ is 'the image of the invisible God' (Col. i.15), an image that reflects the glory of God in his face (II Cor. iv.4–6). Another similar idea is that of a *character*, a perfect impression or stamp, such as might be made by a seal on wax: thus the Epistle to the Hebrews says that Christ 'reflects the glory of God and bears the very stamp of his nature' (i.3). Given this way of speaking, it is natural to go on to describe those who are most Christ-like in such terms, too, for Christian progress is seen as a matter of becoming more and more like Christ. Thus St Paul, again, speaks of those whom God has called as 'destined to be conformed to the image of his Son, in order that he might be the first-born among many brethren' (Rom. viii.29). In this life Christians are acquiring a new nature after the image of their creator (Col. iii.10), in the life to come 'the Lord Jesus Christ . . . will change our lowly body to be like his glorious body' (Phil.iii.20f; cf. I Cor. xv.49). Thus Christ is the mediate image between a restored humanity and God, and the imitation of Christ is the imitation (in the sense of becoming like,[14] rather than slavishly copying) of God. As I have mentioned, there was disagreement among subsequent theologians as to what was lost at the Fall: but whatever it was that was lost was, they agreed, won back for men by Christ. According to Calvin, man is restored through Christ to bear God's image with 'true godliness, righteousness, purity and knowledge' (*Inst.* LXV.4).

There is an important logical relationship implicit in those claims about Christ, namely that of transitivity. It is a characteristic of the relationship of likeness that if *a* is like *b* and if *b* is like *c in the same respects*, then *a* must be like *c* (of course, an image may get successively blurred and a resemblance becomes fainter). So if saintly men are Christ-like, and Christ is the image of God, then, assuming that the likenesses hold in the same respects, saintly men are like God. This elementary logical point has important epistemological implications: for if the saints are in the image of Christ and he is the image of the Father, then the saints reflect some of the glory of the Father. Hence we can come to know something of Him through them.[15]

This knowledge is, it is believed, both of God's nature and of His power: for the saints tell us what God is *like*, and they also tell us of His efficacy, for He has caused them, through the indwelling and transfiguring power of His spirit, to become holy. Now this takes me to the second particular consideration introduced by Christianity, that of the role of the Holy Spirit.

I have already, at the beginning of this chapter, cited St Irenaeus as particularly associating man's likeness to God with the indwelling of the Holy Spirit. Such an association is licensed by II Cor. iii.18 and was made by some other early Fathers. St Cyril of Alexandria, for instance, describes the Holy Spirit as the seal imprinted on the soul to restore its resemblance to God,[16] whose operations consist in 'truly sanctifying and uniting us to Himself, and by conjoining. . .us with Himself makes us partakers of the divine nature'.[17] Moreover, such operations were seen as evidence of the divinity of the Holy Spirit.[18]

Why should the production of a likeness to God be particularly the work of the Holy Spirit? The obvious answer is that he *is* the sanctifying power of God, and so by sanctifying men he makes them like God. We have seen how both in the Old Testament and the New the spirit of God is depicted as the source of sanctification (e.g. Ps li.10f, Rom. xv.16). Putting it another way, we could say that the Holy Spirit brings holiness but holiness is likeness to God, for God is holy.

This answers the question asked. But it is not all that can be said or has been said. For it does not say sufficient about the actual way in which the Holy Spirit works, and it omits to make any connection between his work and that of Christ. As regards the first point, we need to recollect what was said in Chapter 2 about the mode of operation of the Spirit: it is not enough to say that he causes holiness, for we must investigate the nature of a *spiritual* cause. The Holy Spirit is particularly associated with purification and enlightenment: he cleanses the heart and illuminates the minds of rational beings, and thus perfects them.[19] Moreover some have said that the end result of this indwelling is that the spirit of the creature becomes in some sense one with God: St Paul sees the Spirit as himself expressing our prayers within us, bearing united witness to the fatherhood of God (Rom. viii.15f, 26f), whilst William of St Thierry distinguishes a degree of likeness to God which he calls 'unity of spirit', which is much greater than the likeness which consists in virtues, or the likeness all men have in virtue of their creation. Those who enjoy it are made one spirit with God, so that they will only what God wills.[20]

The work of the Holy Spirit is seen in Christian tradition as closely linked with that of Christ, for the Spirit was sent by the Father in Jesus' name, to remind his followers of all he had said, to lead them to the complete truth and to inspire their mission (Jn xiv.26; xvi.13; xx.22). But often the connection is depicted as much more intimate: the New Testament sometimes refers to the Spirit of Jesus,[21] and some early Fathers, for example St Athanasius[22] and St John of Damascus,[23] describe the Holy Spirit as the image of the Son, as the Son is the Father's image. The latter idea is important in the present context, for it suggests that man's likeness to the Father is mediated through both the Son and the Spirit. For if the Spirit is the image of the Son, as the Son is of the Father, then it follows, again through the relationship of transitivity, that through the Spirit man is made in the image of the Father.

Such a way of speaking of the Holy Spirit emerged naturally with the development of Trinitarian Doctrine. For if it is established usage that the Son is the image of the Father, and if the Holy Spirit proceeds from the Father and Son (or from the Father *through* the Son), then it is not surprising if people describe the Spirit too in terms of an 'image'. Such reasoning is based partly on complex theological considerations: in particular, it follows from the claim that within the Trinity the Persons differ only in their relations (of generation, filiation and procession). But there were also other more experiential reasons for the development: Christ's followers felt that he was still amongst them through the presence of the Holy Spirit, because his personality seemed to be manifested in this presence. E. J. Tinsley expresses this very clearly when he writes:

> St. Paul is most aware ... of a life and an activity which is working in and through him moulding him into the shape of the vision of the Image of God which he has seen. This life and activity was the action of the Spirit bringing about the birth of Christ in the Christian, and sustaining the growth of Christ in the believer to maturity. In the Christian *imitatio Christi* the Lord Christ is at one and at the same time the object of the *mimesis* and, through the Spirit, the means of it.[24]

Thus it would seem that in the experience of the early Church there was a close connection between the remembered influence of the earthly Jesus and the continued presence of the Holy Spirit: the latter seemed to remind them not only of what Jesus said (cf. Jn xiv.26) but also of his personality.

THE DESIRE FOR PURIFICATION

I remarked in Chapter 3 that the sanctification of man is usually a gradual process. Thus the likeness to God is wrought only slowly by the Holy Spirit: St Paul says that we 'are being changed into his likeness from one degree of glory to another' (II Cor. iii.18). This process is never completed in this life, so Christian tradition has seen it as continuing in the next. Some, like St Irenaeus, have spoken of the full likeness actually being achieved in the life to come (*Adv. Haer.* v. viii.1); others, like Kant and Hermann Cohen, have seen the attainment of holiness by man as an infinite task which is never completed and therefore requires an endless time in which successive approximations are realised.[25]

Talk of such an attainment may sound rather fanciful, and it naturally suggests a basic question which we have not so far considered: regardless of whether a likeness to God *can* be realised to any degree now or in the life to come, why would anyone want to attain it? Of course there is a familiar religious answer: God created man to be like Himself, to be holy, and our true end is to attain this; moreover Christ has restored the image of God in man, and thereby restored the incorruptibility and immortality lost at the Fall. But this is to see things more from God's point of view. What of man's? What is the context in life in which people talk of likeness to God with 'passion', as Kierkegaard would say, and really come to desire it?

A similar question can be asked about immortality. One can get so bogged down in scriptural exegesis, theological argument and philosophical problems about the possibility of life after death, that one loses sight of the religious point of the discussion. Regardless of whether a life after death is possible or likely, why would anyone want it? Towards the end of his life Mark Twain remarked testily to someone who raised the question of immortality 'Isn't this life enough for you? Do you wish to continue the foolishness somewhere else?'[26] Now Wittgenstein suggests one explanation of how people might come to the idea of immortality: they might feel that they had duties from which they could not be released, even by death.[27] Kant goes a step further in explaining why people might want immortality, in the argument which we have already discussed in an earlier chapter: according to him, holiness (for man) consists in complete fitness of the will to the moral law; but no rational being is capable of such a harmony in this world, although it is a requirement of the practical reason; therefore, it can be achieved only through an infinite progress, that is an infinitely enduring existence and personality of the same rational being.[28]

Now this may suggest a parallel answer to my question about likeness to God: men may become burdened by a sense of their own weakness and unworthiness, and seek purification in the likeness to God and in imitation of Christ. If such a purification is unattainable in this life (to any great degree), then here we have a motive for desiring immortality (which is not the same as an *argument* for its existence). Moreover, we have envisaged a 'form of life' in which a concept of God may arise: God is seen as He whom I should imitate in order to purify myself (cf. 1 Jn iii.3), and also the power which achieves my purification, through His spirit.

This line of thought naturally suggests an obvious objection: is not the God I have mentioned merely an *idea*, one formed as the complement to our desire for purification, a hypostatisation of our

ideals, or a 'projection'? To this objection there are two possible
replies: God is not an idea but a reality who causes things to
happen (in this book I have considered one kind of divine activity,
namely sanctification); and there is a sense in which God is,
indeed, a projection. Normally we think of the term 'projection' as
a derogatory one, as used by Feuerbach and those influenced by
him, for instance, Freud. But such writers had already rejected
belief in God on other grounds (for example they considered that
the concept of God is incoherent), so their claim that the idea of
God is a projection was not designed as a decisive argument for
atheism but as an explanation of how men have come to form the
idea of God.[29] Now if one believes that God has brought man into
being, creating him in His own image and likeness, there is a
perfectly proper sense in which God is a projection. We see what
God is like by looking at our own perfections, imagining them
without any of their flaws and human limitations, and then
projecting them to infinity. This is a procedure which is called the
via remotionis and the *via eminentiae* by Scholastic theologians.
Aquinas, for instance, although anxious to avoid anthropomor-
phising God, thinks that there is a relationship between our
perfections and His, as a consequence of God's creativity. He says
that human perfections have a likeness to God's perfections as
images to an original, and indeed can be said to participate in His
perfections (*S.T.* la.iv.2–3; vi.4; xiii.5–6). The way in which we move
from one to the other is described thus:

> In this life we do not see the essence of God, we only know Him
> from creatures; we think of Him as their source, and then as
> surpassing them all and as lacking anything that is merely
> creaturely. (*S.T.* la.xiii.1 trans. H. McCabe; cf. *De Pot.* vɪɪ.5 ad 3)

The use of the *via remotionis* and also Aquinas' insistence that
perfections pre-exist in God unitedly and simply, whereas in
creatures they are received, divided and multiplied (*S.T.* la. xiii.4)
guarantee that we are not merely projecting a scale of human
qualities and placing God at the final point – as if He simply knows
more and has a higher I.Q. than we have.[30] Aquinas always
emphasises that no creature has a perfection in the same way that
God does, and that the imperfect likeness between creature and
God is not a generic one (ɪ Sent. 22.1.2; *S.T.* la.xiii. 5 ad 2).[31]
Aquinas' procedure goes with a strong doctrine of Creation,

otherwise it would indeed merely be a projection, albeit a very elaborate one. Similarly, the suggestion that our idea of God is among other things an idea of a being who purifies us is only saved from the accusation that it is a projection by some account of the causal role of the Holy Spirit such as I have given in Chapter 2. It was in answer to Feuerbach's charge that the idea of God is merely a projection that von Hügel stressed our experience of the reality of God: he argued that the religious consciousness finds

> an Infinite, *not the soul's own*, present and operative *here and now* in the world and in the soul; an Infinite different in kind from any mere prolongation, since the soul rests on It − on an actually present and operative Perfect Reality. 'On ne s'appuie que sur ce qui résiste,' said Napoleon; we cannot, and indeed do not, lean upon a flux.[32]

Such an appeal to the reality of divine power will only be convinc-ing in so far as one has experienced it for oneself. But one can widen the appeal of considering the saints, as being publicly available examples of those who have been transformed, and therefore as raising the question of *how* they have been transformed.

CONCLUSION

Suppose someone were to ask me what England is like. I might say that it is like France, Holland or some other country in certain respects, but different in others. Then I might show him a map, some photographs and some paintings, like Constable's *Dedham Vale*, or perhaps play some English music, like one of Elgar's symphonies, in order to try to convey some idea of our national spirit.

What is God like? I might first of all try to answer this question by providing a theological definition. But this would not actually answer it, for it would not say *to what* God is *like*. My respondent might demand 'Show me!' Then, as a Christian, I might point to Jesus Christ. But I might also point to the saints either in their own right, or because they are in the likeness of Christ. In the latter case the logical point I have raised with regard to the relation of transitivity would be important. If the saints are like Christ, and he is like the Father, then it follows that we can know of the Father through the saints. This relationship is perhaps better expressed if we use the term 'image' because it conveys the causal priority: if the saints are in the image of Christ, and he is *the* image of the Father, then the saints reflect some of the glory of the Father.

How is the likeness to God produced? By purifying oneself, walking in the ways of God and imitating Christ. But Christians believe that these things are only possible through the power of the Holy Spirit, and that the saints are outstanding examples of those who have been stamped by the power of God's spirit in the likeness of His son.

6   Conclusion

The idea of likeness to God has given us a further answer to the question raised at the beginning of this book, of why the indwelling of the Holy Spirit is an anticipation of the life to come: this answer is that the Holy Spirit renews the likeness of God in men and women, and so prepares them for the time when they will be wholly like Him (in so far as this is possible). This claim, of course, is not independent of what has been said in earlier chapters, for it too relies on the notion of the spirit of God and His works, and it appeals to certain assumptions about God's power, promise and fidelity which I have previously discussed.

The argument of this book has two limitations: it depends on certain theological assumptions, and it deals with only one aspect of religion, what is conveniently termed 'spirituality'. The reliance on assumptions is inevitable in any theological work, and is legitimate, provided that they are brought out into the open and that the logical structure of the arguments in which they are involved is clear. In general, my strategy in this work has been to point to something which is, to some extent, visible to all, spiritual renewal, and to show how, if this is regarded as being brought about by one mode of God's action, His working through men's hearts by His spirit, it is brought into a wide-ranging interpretive and explanatory scheme. In particular, it may be connected with belief in immortality, given certain assumptions (which I have indicated) about God's promises, fidelity and power. The second limitation I have mentioned is also inevitable, given that one cannot cover every subject all the time. It does, however, present us with a real question: what is the relationship between God's inspiration and permeation of men through His spirit and His creative power in nature? The presence of God's spirit in the hearts of men is only one form of divine presence and activity. As I have remarked elsewhere, one may acknowledge God's spiritual power in one's own life, in a religious community or in the lives of the saints, and yet wonder about His presence in a poverty-stricken and disease-ridden world.[1] A partial answer, but only a partial one, is that God works in the world mainly through secondary causes, and that His inspiration of men through the Holy Spirit is the most important way in which He works out His purposes in the world.

A further more particular limitation is that the 'first fruits' argument for immortality which I considered in Chapter 4 is only one of many considerations which incline men to belief in a life after death. This, again, is not of great significance, since obviously I am not claiming that this is the *only* argument for immortality; it is just that it is the one most relevant to my subject, and also, as it happens, the one which has attracted least attention, at least in recent times. It is, however, true that it raises two questions, which are in fact raised by any argument for immortality, and which I have not yet considered. It presupposes that the idea of immortality is coherent, that is, that the idea of a life after death makes sense; and it does not say sufficient about the point or purpose of such a life. I will say a little about these two important objections before drawing some more general conclusions.

THE POSSIBILITY AND PURPOSE OF IMMORTALITY

It is no use speculating about the nature of life after death or investigating arguments about it, whether philosophical or theological, if in fact the idea of such a life is incoherent. In particular, we must show that there are criteria of identity whereby a resurrected body or a disembodied soul could be shown to be the same person as the earthly man or woman whose life it supposedly continues.

Much of the writing in English on the subject of immortality in the last ten years or so has been inspired by Terence Penelhum's book *Survival and Disembodied Existence*, which raises the questions of identity to which I have alluded. Penelhum enquires first of all into the notion of survival of disembodied souls, and finds difficulties in this. He raises an objection which I have already mentioned in Chapter 2, of whether it makes sense to speak of such souls 'seeing', 'doing' and so on. Then he asks how a disembodied soul could be identified with a *pre-mortem* person, and denies that memory alone could serve as a principle of identity, because memory must be capable of being checked, and any checking procedure would have to appeal to considerations of physical identity (for instance, of whether someone really was present at an event he or she claims to remember). Penelhum concludes that belief in a bodily resurrection has fewer logical difficulties than belief in disembodied survival, but even this raises a question of identity: for what reason would there be to identify the resurrected person with the *pre-mortem* one, once you have eliminated the idea of an immaterial soul as the principle of continuity in the interim period between death and resurrection? It *seems* reasonable to do so, yet there is no argument which we could offer to someone who refused to do so and insisted that the resurrected person would be only a replica (the argument is sharpened if one envisages the possibility of multiple replication of a single person[2]).

In order to refute charges that the notion of immortality is incoherent it is necessary only to show that *one* form of immortality is logically possible. Most contemporary philosophers have chosen to defend the notion of bodily resurrection rather than disembodied survival (though Professor H. D. Lewis, for example, thinks the latter is defensible). Some have argued that human beings may be 'gappy' entities like plays or television-serials (an analogy mentioned by Penelhum), which by their very nature do not have a continuous and uninterrupted history. If so, there could be good grounds for claiming a continued identity: provided that there was only one claimant to re-embodiment in the next world per earthly person, then we might decide that each claimant *was* the same as the earthly person, not because of an arbitrary decision but because the identity claims would be based on the criteria of similarity of body and character, and continuity of memory.[3] Other philosophers have maintained belief in bodily resurrection on more traditional lines, contending that the conception of an interim stage of disembodied existence between death and resurrection can be defended against the arguments of Penelhum and others. Paul Helm, for instance, thinks that there is nothing incoherent in the idea of a 'minimal person' surviving death and then remembering, thinking, reasoning and having dream-like perceptions. He regards memory as *evidence* for identity, rather than as constituting it, for a lack of memory would not entail a lack of identity. The fact that memory-claims are checkable by physical tests, and therefore conflicts between them are resolved by such checks, does not show that memory by itself is *no* evidence. After all, there are some memory claims in the embodied state that cannot be checked. The 'minimal person' would merely lack the inductive support for his memory-claims that is gained from physical checking.[4]

Helm's line of argument is closer to the 'two-stage' view of many traditional Christian theologians, like Aquinas, than is that of Hick, Reichenbach and Young. I will not seek to adjudicate between them, since I think that they have all succeeded in providing an adequate defence of the notion of bodily resurrection. More to my purpose now is to enquire about the *point* of such a survival after death. It is possible, in principle, that men might rise from the dead to continue the same kind of life that they have led on earth, or to live a crudely hedonistic life, as envisaged in some primitive myths. But what would be the moral or religious point of such after-lives?

The question of the point of an after-life really divides up into two questions: (i) why do (or should) religious people desire to be immortal? (ii) why would God want men to be immortal?

As regards the first question, I have already mentioned that one can envisage future lives without any particularly moral or religious features. There is nothing specifically religious about a desire for immortality. It is natural to desire to rejoin loved ones, to pursue continued happiness and hope for a reward (especially if one feels that life in this world has been too full of suffering or has dealt unfairly with one). Of course, not all people have desired these things: in the last chapter I quoted Mark Twain's testy remark in the matter, and in his 'The Makropoulos Case' Bernard Williams remarks on the unbearable tedium of some after-lives which are envisaged merely as continuations of this life.[5] The point was put more wittily by George Gershwin in *Porgy and Bess*:

> Methusaleh lived nine hundred years
> But who calls dat livin'
> When no gal will give in
> To no man what's nine hundred years.

At this point we have to remind ourselves of some of the things that have been said in previous chapters about the demand for complete holiness, the desire for purification and for likeness to God, and the witness of the saints who are seen as pioneers on the road to holiness. Religious people do not wish simply for survival after death, for 'more of the same'; rather, they wish for something higher and better. They desire, first of all, to be with God, to continue the love and worship of Him, and to know Him more intimately; and then to be changed by this encounter so that they achieve true holiness; and also to be in the fellowship of other children of God.

The traditional term for this more intimate knowledge of God is 'The Beatific Vision', a term coined to describe the state envisaged by St Paul when he says 'For now we see in a mirror dimly, but then face to face. Now I know in part; then I shall understand fully' (I Cor. xiii.12). Some mystics, for instance St John of the Cross,[6] have seen their experience as an anticipation of heaven; and it has been argued that some types of mystical experience may give us an imaginative 'schema' of what is to come, for in them there is a sense of union with God, with no awareness of space or time, but with a sense of peace and harmony. Mystical experience is a more intense kind of experience, yet one which is regarded by those who enjoy it as but a shadow of what is to come, of our true goal.[7]

This relationship between the Beatific Vision and mystical experience may well hold, but we do need to supplement what has been said about it by considering the dimensions of community and of personal growth. To do justice to the concept of the 'Communion of Saints' we must hypothesise some form of fellowship in the life to come (of course, some mystics have spoken of a sense of communion with all creatures, as well as with God, in this life). And what has been said about the desire for purification and holiness requires that we do not simply consider the *experience* of the Beatific Vision, for the Christian tradition also teaches that we shall *be* transformed: 'Beloved, we are God's children now; it does not yet appear what we shall be, but we know that when he appears we shall be like him, for we shall see him as he is' (I Jn iii.2). In the life to come there will be completeness, healing and purification. Some have seen this transformation as being achieved instantaneously; others have envisaged it as a gradual process which continues in the age to come, perhaps requiring an everlasting life in which we asymptotically approach an infinite goal (I have already mentioned St Gregory of Nyssa, Kant, Hermann Cohen and Unamuno in this connection, but Brightman and A. E. Taylor are further examples of writers who have envisaged the future life as a moral progress or eternal growth, with continued learning, activity and loving).[8]

These answers to the question of why religious people might desire immortality throw some light on the second question, of why God might desire men to be immortal. Putting the matter negatively we might ask why a loving God would create people *not* to be immortal? For if death is the end for them, then their 'immortal longings', particularly their desire to continue to know God and to be with Him, will be frustrated; and more importantly, their potentiality for transformation through God's grace into a likeness of Him will be unrealised. This is, of course, to see things from man's point of view. Nevertheless, the decisive consideration is God's love for us: one expects such a love to have a regard for people's aspirations and for their growth towards perfection (of course, further arguments may be adduced by considering His justice, for example that a just God would require men to reap what they have sown).

One could pursue this line of thought further by asking whether it tells us anything about the nature of the life to come. Christians might argue that a loving God, who came to us in human need and human love in the Incarnation, would not frustrate our desire to meet our loved ones again. If grace perfects nature, then this includes the perfection of our natural ties of family, love and friendship. But if the future life is to be a social one, then this in turn suggests again that it will also be one of bodily resurrection rather than disembodied existence.[9] Thus the Christian doctrines of the Communion of the Saints and the Resurrection of the Body are confirmed by further considerations. But all this is, I think, somewhat more speculative: Christ's words that the risen 'neither marry nor are given in marriage, but are like angels in heaven' (Mk xii.25) should warn us of the danger of projecting our current ideas of community on to the next world. Still, I think that it is legitimate to try to specify, in the most general terms, some of the characteristics of the life to come in terms of its religious purpose. H. Wheeler Robinson is surely right that 'the content of the life beyond must be thought out in terms of the Spirit-transformed life here'.[10] And this suggests, according to him, that it will involve individuality, but also fellowship, and a moral continuity in which there is growth towards perfection and in the knowledge of God.

THE IMPORTANCE OF THE SAINTS

The main conclusion to be drawn from my discussion is that the existence of saintly people is a much more important fact than is usually realised. In particular, it is crucial for Christianity that such people should continue to arise in every generation. It is important from a devotional point of view, for the saints, as people growing in the image of Christ, are continual reminders of what it is to be Christ-like. As the Abbé Huvelin puts it, they are 'living images painted by Christ himself for his Church that he might recall some of his own features to her mind and console her in her widowhood'.[11] In them we see the transfiguring power of holiness, anticipating resurrection. But the existence of saints is also important from a philosophical point of view, as being one of the factors relevant to an assessment of the truth-claims of Christianity, for they have an evidential role: they are evidence for the presence and power of the Holy Spirit; and so, conversely, the absence of saintliness may tend to count against the truth of Christianity.[12] Their existence is also evidence for immortality, given certain theological assumptions. These considerations about the devotional and evidential importance of sanctity are independent of more disputed considerations concerning the propriety of praying to the saints, their powers of intercession, the application of their 'merits' to the salvation of others, the veneration of relics and tombs, canonisation and so on.[13]

It is unfortunate, therefore, that devotion to the saints has declined within Christianity in recent decades, and that there has been relatively little theological consideration of their role. Of course, the relative lack of consideration of the question within Protestantism is not surprising, for it is a relic of the Reformers' attack on what they regarded as abuses in the Roman practices of devotion to the saints and on the prerogatives claimed by the Papacy in canonisation. But the Reformers did not discount the importance of sanctification. Calvin was much concerned with the 'new life' of holiness, the essential inner and outer transformation of the justified; he said 'We never dream either of a faith destitute of good works or of a justification unattended by them . . . Christ therefore justifies no one whom he does not also sanctify' (*Inst.* III.xvi.1). Although Luther saw devotion to the saints as tending to detract from the uniqueness of Christ, he hailed the persecuted

and martyred evangelical Christians of the Netherlands as 'real
saints'. Michael Perham correctly says of him:

> Like Calvin, his quarrel was with false saints and with false
> honour to saints, not with the idea that some men and women
> can be held up as special examples of the grace of God at
> work.[14]

Within Roman Catholicism there has recently been a widespread
decline in devotion to the saints. This cannot, I think, be ascribed
to the influence of the Second Vatican Council, since §50 of *Lumen
Gentium*, from which I quoted in Chapter 3, gives a brief but
beautiful and accurate account of their importance; and the whole
of Chapter v of that constitution deals with the question of
holiness being a goal which all Christians should pursue. It is more
likely that the decline is due to other factors: a reaction against too
many exaggerated devotions and statues in bad taste, and a desire
to reassert the primacy of Jesus Christ as *the* mediator between
God and man (but again, it needs to be pointed out that if saintly
people are seen as *images* of him, then they are not supplanting
him, nor does respect paid to them detract from worship of him).
It is likely, too, that a more chastened devotion to them will
reassert itself, if the Roman Catholic church moves into a more
settled period, following the turbulence of the post-Vatican II
years. The Orthodox churches have always maintained a strong
tradition of devotion to the saints.[15]

The relative neglect of the topic by philosophers is less explic-
able, for presumably not all of them are so powerfully affected by
movements for religious reform and by theological fashion.
Perhaps they feel that the phenomenon of sanctity is susceptible of
a naturalistic explanation: but if so, the question does at least need
to be argued out. Or perhaps they feel that the subject is one
exclusively for theologians. I have, however, tried to indicate that
there are interesting and important philosophical problems to be
considered. Philosophers too should marvel at the existence of the
saints, and ask themselves the question: if in a dedicated religious
life people come to have certain experiences and to be changed in
various ways, what does this show? In this book I have looked at
one answer. But those who approach this question, whether philosophers or theologians, should do so with the sober realisation

that it is easier to think and to write about holiness than to attain it.

Notes

CHAPTER 1:   Introduction

1. *On the Holy Spirit*, Works of John Wesley (4th edn, London, 1840) Vol. VII, p.490. I am indebted to Mr Jerry Walls for this reference.
2. Karl Rahner, 'The Church of the Saints', in *Theological Investigations*, Vol. III, trans. K. H. and B. Kruger (London, 1967), p.104. Elsewhere he speaks of grace anticipating glory and the Beatific Vision, for example in 'The Concept of Mystery in Catholic Theology', *Theological Investigations* Vol. IV, trans. K. Smyth (London, 1966), pp.54, 56.
3. Vladimir Lossky, *The Mystical Theology of the Eastern Church* (London, 1957), p.179; cf. p.230.
4. See Andrew Louth, *Theology and Spirituality* (Fairacres, 1976), p.3. Such a definition requires qualification when we come to consider non-theistic religions.
5. See further my *Religion, Truth and Language-Games* (London, 1977), pp. 112f.
6. F. Crosson, in C. F. Delaney (ed.) *Religion and Rationality* (London and Notre Dame, 1979), p.154.
7. G. Curtis, in his introduction to M. Chavchavadze (ed.), *Man's Concern with Holiness* (London, 1970), p.13.
8. For example in F. von Hügel, *Letters to a Niece* (London, 1928), p.xxxvi.
9. John Henry Newman, *Apologia pro Vita Sua* (Everyman edn, London, 1955), p.150.
10. Ian Ramsey, 'Theology Today and Spirituality Today', in Eric James (ed.), *Spirituality for Today* (London, 1968), p.76.
11. S. Bolshakoff and M. B. Pennington, *In Search of True Wisdom: Visits to Eastern Spiritual Fathers* (New York, 1979), p.88. See Lossky, *Mystical Theology . . .*, Ch. 1, for similar remarks about the role of theology.
12. See Paul Holmer, *The Grammar of Faith* (San Francisco, 1978), especially Chs. 4 and 9.
13. Kenneth Leech, *Soul Friend* (London, 1977), pp.35f.
14. Thomas Merton, *New Seeds of Contemplation* (London, 1962), pp.197f.
15. Hans Urs von Balthasar, in *Word and Redemption* (New York, 1965), Chs 3–4. These essays are translated from his *Verbum Caro. Skizzen zur Theologie*, I, part 2.

CHAPTER 2:   The Spirit of God

1. R. Bultmann, 'New Testament and Mythology', in H. W. Bartsch (ed.),

Kerygma and Myth, Vol. 1 (London, 1953), p.5. James Dunn observes of this passage: 'The trouble is, of course, that "the New Testament world of demons and spirits" is also the biblical world of the Holy Spirit' ('Rediscovering the Spirit (2)', in *Expository Times*, xCIV (1982), 11).

2. See Karl Rahner, *Theological Investigations*, Vol. v (London, 1966), p.162; *Hominisation: The Evolutionary Origin of Man as a Theological Problem* (London, 1965), pp.46–61.
3. See also Richard Swinburne, *The Existence of God* (Oxford, 1979), p.8.
4. Paul Edwards, 'Difficulties in the Idea of God', in E. Madden, R. Handy and M. Farber (eds), *The Idea of God* (Springfield, Illinois, 1968), p.48.
5. Antony Flew, *The Presumption of Atheism* (London, 1976), p.141.
6. Antony Flew, *God and Philosophy* (London, 1966), pp.32f; *The Presumption of Atheism* (London,1976), p.147. Similar objections are made by Kai Nielsen, in *Contemporary Critiques of Religion* (London, 1971), Ch. 6, and by T. Penelhum, in *Survival and Disembodied Existence* (London, 1970), Chs 6 and 10. The latter answers the problem of how we would identify an incorporeal being by making the heroic suggestion that perhaps there may be only one such, namely God.
7. This is somewhat along the lines of Descartes' argument for the existence of incorporeal substances in his reply to Hobbes' objections to the *Meditations* (*Oeuvres*, ed. Adam & Tannery, VII, Paris, 1964, pp.175–6.) I take it that such arguments are an application of the mediaeval principle *operari sequitur esse*.
8. Locke treats the term 'spirit' somewhat like that of 'animal': he envisages a whole hierarchy of different kinds of spirit, with God at the apex. The idea of God is distinguished from that of other spirits by His infinity (*Essay* III.vi.11–12).
9. Antony Flew, *The Presumption of Atheism*, p.154, in answer to P. F. Strawson, *Individuals* (London, 1959), pp.115f.
10. Immanuel Kant, *Dreams of a Spirit Seer*, Acad. ed. Vol.II, pp.319, 321.
11. O. Marquard shows that even before the rise of Idealism *Geist* was used to cover *mens, anima, génie, esprit*, evil genius, the Holy Spirit, *genius loci*, familiar spirit, earth-spirit, and the spirit of an age, nation or the world. See J. Ritter (ed.), *Historisches Wörterbuch der Philosophie*, Band 3 (Darmstadt, 1974), column 185.
12. Donald Evans, 'Commentary on Paul Edwards' Paper', in E. Madden, R. Handy and M. Farber, *Idea of God*, p.84. Evans also gives the parallel of poltergeists, as does Swinburne in the passage already mentioned in which he is discussing the concept of an omnipresent spirit. To be fair, Swinburne, following Aquinas, does justice to God's presence *in* things through His creative power. But again, there is no reference to religious concepts of prayer, conversion, and so on here.
13. Aquinas, interestingly enough, uses the term relatively rarely of God, perhaps because his mentor Aristotle does not use it of his Unmoved Mover, perhaps because such a use might give the impression, which Locke perhaps gives, that God is a member of a genus which also includes angels, human souls, evil spirits, etc., and Aquinas is emphatic that God is outside of every genus (*S.T.* Ia.iii.5).
14. The other plausible candidate is II Cor. iii.17f. But the context shows that the passage may assert an identity between the Lord revered by the Jews and

the Spirit of the living God. See further J. D. G. Dunn, '2 Corinthians III.17 – "The Lord is the Spirit" ', *Journal of Theological Studies* (1970), pp.309–20.

15. This is not to say that we cannot continue to use the term 'a spirit', for there are plenty of Biblical references specifying a particular spirit by using the definite article, as well as ones using the plural *pneumata*.

16. C. H. Dodd calls it a 'most gross perversion of the meaning' to translate it as 'God is a Spirit', for this implies that there is a class of *pneumata*, an idea alien to the Fourth Gospel (*The Interpretation of the Fourth Gospel*, Cambridge 1953, p.225). In general, I myself do not think that it is a *mistake* to describe God as a spirit, if by that is meant that He is an immaterial and intelligent agent. It is just that such a description loses, as we shall see, a lot of the richness of the Biblical usage of the term.

17. Origen, *Cels.* VI.70; *De Principiis* I.1–4; *Commentary on St. John*, XIII.23. See also St Gregory of Nyssa, *Eun.* VII, for a warning against understanding 'spirit', or 'Lord', as God's essence.

18. See Marie Isaacs, *The Concept of Spirit: A Study of Pneuma in Hellenistic Judaism and its Bearing on the New Testament* (London, 1976) Appendix D, for a useful classification of the N.T. uses.

19. Geoffrey Lampe, *God as Spirit* (Oxford, 1977).

20. There is often, of course, a similar play on words in the New Testament, for instance, in John iii.8 and xx.22. We must never lose sight of the fact that in origin 'spirit' is a metaphorical term.

21. See Acts x.38; I Cor. ii.4; and I Thess. i.5 for the hendiadys 'power and spirit'.

22. See Bartsch, *Kerygma and Myth*, p.6. What is particularly lacking here is a consideration of the way in which God is believed to work through 'secondary causes', that is the ordinary course of events. If God's providence is believed to work in this way, then presumably His inspiration can act through our ordinary mental processes. See further John Shepherd, 'The Concept of Revelation', *Religious Studies*, 16 (1980), 425–37, also John V. Taylor's comment: 'The writings of most of the Pentecostalists and other revivalists that I have read seem to me to look upon the Holy Spirit too much as a supply of superhuman power and wisdom and so to miss the fact that he works primarily by generating awareness and communion, and that whatever power and wisdom he gives derive from that' (*The Go-Between God*, London, 1972, p.200).

23. R. Bultmann, *Theology of the New Testament* (London, 1952), Vol. I, §§14,38.

24. See further my article 'Philosophy and the Saints', *Heythrop Journal* (January 1977), especially 25f. Similarly, the claim to have been guided by the Holy Spirit is often a *post facto* judgement, based on the outcome of decisions and actions.

25. See E. Schweizer (ed.), *Spirit of God* (London, 1960), pp.82f.

26. Bultmann attributes these differences in language to the fact that the New Testament has two concepts of the Holy Spirit: (i) an animistic concept, of an independent, personal agent; (ii) a dynamistic concept, of an impersonal force which fills a man like a fluid (*Theology of the New Testament*, Vol. I §14).

27. One might, I think, argue that the fact that both personal and impersonal predicates are applied to the Spirit simply makes him a different kind of person from human persons: after all, the latter have two kinds of predicates applied to them, namely those appropriate only to persons, for example 'is thinking hard' or 'is in pain', and those also used of inanimate objects, for example 'weighs ten stone' (cf. Strawson, op.cit. pp.104–10). So might it not be the case that spirits likewise have two sets of predicates, namely those appropriate to persons and the others which I have mentioned?

28. Ian Crombie, in B. Mitchell (ed.), *Faith and Logic* (London, 1957), pp.31–83.

29. See Kai Nielsen, 'On Fixing the Reference Range of God', *Religious Studies* II (1966–7), pp.21–5, and M. Durrant, *The Logical Status of 'God'* (London, 1973), p.13.

30. Similar considerations led the early nineteenth-century Roman Catholic theologian, J. A. Möhler, to insist, against Schleiermacher, that the Holy Spirit cannot be *only* the common feeling of Christians, for people have worshipped the Holy Spirit since ancient times, and 'Who would worship the common feeling?' (unedited ms. for his *Einheit*, quoted in Donald J. Dietrich, *The Goethezeit and the Metamorphosis of Catholic Theology in the Age of Idealism*, European University Studies, XXIII, 128 (Berne, 1979), p.141).

31. Keith Ward, *The Concept of God* (Oxford, 1974), p.215.

32. C. Jung, *Modern Man in Search of a Soul* (London, 1933), pp.258f.

33. Swinburne, as we have seen, distinguishes between the identity of a thing in itself, which he says is ultimate, and our means of identifying it. My remarks here are concerned with the latter. I take it that the doctrine of the Trinity is an attempt to explain the former in the case of the Holy Spirit.

34. This criterion was an important influence on one aspect of Hegel's concept of spirit, as I Cor. ii. 10f, cited earlier, influenced another aspect.

35. David Hume, *Dialogues on Natural Religion* VI, Kemp Smith edn, p.171.

36. Though, as we have seen, he does not think that 'spirit' and 'body' are incompatible. Similarly, in his letter to the Bishop of Worcester, Locke says that 'spirit' denotes thought and active motion, and is not necessarily immaterial (*Works*, 12th edn, London, 1824, Vol. III, pp.34f).

37. Christopher Stead suggests that the term can be applied to God in this minimal sense. See his *Divine Substance* (Oxford, 1977), pp.271–3.

38. See John Hick, *Faith and Knowledge* (2nd edn, London, 1967), especially Ch. 5; and 'Religious Faith as Experiencing as', in G. Vesey (ed.), *Talk of God*, Royal Institute of Philosophy Lectures, Vol. II (London, 1969).

39. James Dunn, *Jesus and the Spirit* (London, 1975), p.47 (his italics).

40. Among the many recent books on the Holy Spirit, Louis Bouyer's *Le Consolateur: Esprit-Saint et vie de Grâce* (Paris, 1980), especially Part I, is most helpful in explaining this development and relating the doctrine of the Holy Spirit to that of the Trinity. He remarks that the Western Church for many centuries lost any sense of the activity of the Holy Spirit as such because, following St Augustine, it came to think that the three Persons always act in relation to the world as a single principle and that it is only by 'appropria- tion' that we can ascribe actions in the world to any one of them. Hence the Holy Spirit became the 'unknown God', and the theology of the Holy Spirit was supplanted by that of grace.

CHAPTER 3:   Saints

1. *On the Holy Spirit* (Christian Classics series, trans. G. Lewis, London, n.d.), §§46, 48.
2. John Oman accused Rudolph Otto of giving insufficient attention to this in his *The Idea of the Holy*. See O. R. Jones, *The Concept of Holiness* (London, 1961), Ch. VIII, for a discussion of the dispute.
3. *Early Christian Writings*, trans. Maxwell Staniforth (Harmondsworth, 1968), p.193.
4. F. von Hügel, *The Mystical Element of Religion* (London, 1923), Vol. I, p.107. For von Hügel's contribution to the questions discussed in this book, see my 'Von Hügel: Philosophy and Spirituality', *Religious Studies*, XVII (1981), 1–18.
5. Aelred Squire, *Asking the Fathers* (London, 1973), p.179.
6. *Lumen Gentium* (Constitution on the Church) §50, in W. Abbott and J. Gallagher (eds), *The Documents of Vatican II* (London, 1966) p.82.
7. Henri de Lubac, *The Church, Paradox and Mystery*, trans. James R. Dunne, (Shannon, 1969), p.126.
8. F. von Hügel, *Selected Letters 1896–1924*, B. Holland (ed.) (London, 1927), pp.266, 301.
9. See further Lawrence Cunningham, *The Meaning of Saints* (San Francisco, 1980), pp.73–5.
10. Richard Swinburne, *Faith and Reason* (Oxford, 1981), pp.59f.
11. Quoted in K. Leech, *Soul Friend* (London, 1977), p.48. On Amvrosy see further S. Bolshakoff, *Russian Mystics* (London, 1977), Ch. IX. He served as one of the models for Fr Zossima in Dostoievski's *The Brothers Karamazov*.
12. Karl Rahner, *Theological Investigations*, Vol. III (London, 1967), p.94.
13. From the memorandum inaugurating the series *The Lives of the Saints*, in V. F. Blehl (ed.) *The Essential Newman* (New York, 1963), p.334.
14. H. H. Price, in his *Belief* (London, 1969), pp.474ff. See my *Religion, Truth and Language-Games* (London, 1977), pp.110f, and 'Philosophy and the Saints' *Heythrop Journal*, XVIII (1977), pp.30–2, for an exposition and critique of Price's argument.
15. Antonia White, *The Hound and the Falcon* (London, 1965), p.73. See William James, *The Varieties of Religious Experience*, Lectures XIV–XV for similar examples; he explains them by suggesting that saintly attributes like devoutness, purity, charity and asceticism may run into error by excess. See also Cunningham, *The Meaning of Saints*, Ch. 2 for a discussion of the issues raised.
16. *The Babylonian Captivity of the Church*, in J. Dillenberger (ed.) *Martin Luther: Selections from his Writings* (Garden City, N.Y., 1961), p.311. It should be noted that Luther is not *condemning* monasticism but saying it is no higher than the other callings mentioned. Nevertheless, it almost disappeared from Protestantism for over three centuries.
17. G. F. Moore, *Judaism*, vol. II (Harvard, 1927), p.265. Although Judaism is opposed to monasticism and celibacy it does allow a role to fasting and penitential disciplines. Buddhism encourages asceticism, but for a different reason from Christianity: it rejects the world because it is transitory rather than because it may be a source of sin. The Buddha says: 'If only this beauty of women were imperishable then my mind would certainly indulge in the passions' (quoted by John Passmore, in *The Perfectibility of Man*

(London, 1970), p.125.

18. See Peter Geach, 'An Irrelevance of Omnipotence', *Philosophy*, 48, no. 186 (Oct. 1973) 333.

19. See William James, *Varieties of Religious Experience* (Fontana edn, London, 1960), pp.323f.

20. I will pass by the interesting question of supererogation; the difference between regarding something as obligatory and as highly commendable but beyond the range of duty. See J. O. Urmson, 'Saints and Heroes', in I. A. Melden (ed.), *Essays in Moral Philosophy* (Seattle, 1958), pp.198–216.

21. Thomas Merton, *No Man is an Island* (London, 1955), pp.198, 225.

22. J.-P. Sartre, *Sketch for a Theory of the Emotions* (trans. Philip Mairet, London, 1962), p.91. See Leslie Stevenson, *Seven Theories of Human Nature* (Oxford, 1974), Ch. 7 for a discussion of Sartre's views and Rollo May, *Love and Will* (London, 1970), especially Chs 9–11, for an application to love. Errol Bedford's 'Emotions' (*Proceedings of the Aristotelian Society*, LVII, 1956–7, 281–304) is also an important discussion. Robert C. Neville discusses the training of desires, arguing that one can control the extent to which a thing is allowed to be important within one's experience: see his *Soldier, Sage, Saint* (New York, 1978), especially pp.75–83.

23. Fr A. Yelchaninov, *Fragments of a Diary* (London, 1967), p.111.

24. K. Leech, *Soul Friend* (London, 1977), p.64, paraphrasing Augustine Baker.

25. See further my *Religion, Truth and Language-Games* (London, 1977), pp.5–8, 112f for a fuller discussion of Wittgenstein's thought here and of its implications for spirituality.

26. William James, *Varieties of Religious Experience*, pp.486–94.

27. Maurice Wiles sees this in his *The Remaking of Christian Doctrine* (London, 1974), Ch. 5, but in his anxiety to stress that there is no need to look for 'some special supernatural causation' (p.102) he neglects to consider the concept of secondary causality.

28. This would also apply to many scientific entities. Dorothy Emmet tells an amusing story: 'My friend Catherine Hoskins when a small girl once went to a party at the Braggs, and said afterwards to Richard Braithwaite "Uncle Richard, Professor Bragg has been showing us electrons", and he said, "Nonsense, child, an electron is a theoretical construct" ' ('Haunted Universes', *Second Order*, January 1972, p.35).

29. Immanuel Kant, *Religion within the Bounds of Reason Alone*, Bk. IV, Pt.ii; trans. T. M. Greene and H. T. Hudson (New York, 1960), pp.162, 179f.

30. F. von Hügel, *Essays and Addresses in the Philosophy of Religion*, Vol. II (London, 1926), p.22.

31. Grover Maxwell, 'The Ontological Status of Theoretical Entities' in *Minnesota Studies in the Philosophy of Science*, Vol. III (Minneapolis, 1962), pp.3–27.

32. Kai Nielsen, 'God and Postulated Entities', *Southern Journal of Philosophy*, XII (1974), 225–30. See also his 'Empiricism, Theoretical Constructs and God', *Journal of Religion*, LIV (1974), 199–217, and ' "Christian Positivism" and the Appeal to Religious Experience', *Journal of Religion*, XLII (1962) 248-61.

33. We must be on our guard here against taking too simplistic a view of scientific procedure: not all theories are rejected when they are apparently falsified (see R. Swinburne, 'Falsifiability of Scientific Theories', *Mind* n.s. LXXIII (1964) 434–6), and scientists use other criteria besides verifiability and

falsifiability, for example simplicity, coherence and comprehensiveness.

34. My argument at this point owes much to Richard Swinburne, *The Existence of God* (Oxford, 1979).

35. See, for example, Karl Rahner, 'Nature and Grace' in his *Theological Investigations*, Vol. IV (trans. Kevin Smyth, London, 1974), Ch. 7.

36. Sermon 76, Ch. 3 (*P.L.* liv:405f). Ch. 4 of de Lubac, *Church, Paradox and Mystery*, gives other such examples, both from the Fathers and from modern writers.

37. The question of what the existence of saintly Buddhists *is evidence for* is more difficult: it might well seem patronising or arrogant for a Christian to claim that they show forth the workings of divine grace, given that they them-selves might well say that it merely showed the effectiveness of the Eightfold Path and their spiritual discipline. Yet the claim might be true. In any case, Mahayana Buddhism tends more towards a doctrine of grace in its recogni-tion of the Buddha as a saviour and of the role of Bodhisattvas. See Ninian Smart, *The Religious Experience of Mankind* (Fount Paperback edn, London, 1977), pp.134f, 144.

38. Martin Luther, *Preface to the Epistle of St. Paul to the Romans*, in Dillenberger, *Selections from his Writings*, pp.23–4. See R. Prenter, 'Holiness in the Lutheran Tradition', in M. Chavchavadze (ed.), *Man's Concern with Holiness* (London, 1970), for further discussion of such passages; and J. W. Beardslee 'Sanctifica-tion in Reformed Theology' in J. Meyendorff and J. McLelland (eds), *The New Man* (New Brunswick, N.J., 1973), for Calvin's position.

CHAPTER 4:   First Fruits

1. Assuming, with Chrysostom and Augustine, that Paul is referring here to the final resurrection and not to the continual operations of the Spirit in us here and now. See C. E. B. Cranfield, *A Critical and Exegetical Commentary in the Epistle to the Romans*, Vol. I (Edinburgh 1975), p.391.

2. I prefer this old fashioned term to modern translations like 'pledge' or 'guarantee', since, as we shall see, it is closer to the meaning of the original Greek term *arrabōn*. The phrases 'first instalment' or 'down payment' are also closer in meaning (though some people may dislike their connotations of buying washing machines, etc.!).

3. *Midrash Rabbah*, Vol. III *Exodus*, H. Freedman and M. Simon (eds), trans. S. M. Lehrman (London, 1939), p.551. See Wis. VI. 18–19 for wisdom bringing assurance of immortality.

4. Trans. G. G. Walsh in *Fathers of the Church*, Vol. VII (New York, 1949), p.52. Other examples I have found are: Irenaeus, *Adv. Haer.* v.vii.1f., xiii.4. *Epideixis* 42; Theodore of Mopsuestia, *On Baptism* in *Woodbrooke Studies*, Vol. VI, A. Mingana (ed.) (Cambridge, 1933), pp.54, 56, 75.

5. *C.D.* IV i.p.308. I am not sure that all the New Testament passages which he quotes bear the sense he wishes to give them, for example Rom. i.4, I Tim. iii.16 and I Pet. iii.18.

6. Josiah Royce, *The Conception of Immortality* (Boston and New York, 1900), pp.84ff.

7. Louis Dupré, *Transcendent Selfhood* (New York, 1976), p.80.

8. C. H. Dodd, *The Interpretation of the Fourth Gospel* (Cambridge, 1953), p.148, cf. also p.364.
9. *Adv. Haer.* v.xiii.4, trans. A. Roberts and W. H. Rambaut in *The Writings of Irenaeus*, Vol.II (Edinburgh, 1869), p.90.
10. Though it has been argued that some religious statements can be verified in this life or the next: see J. Hick, 'Theology and Verification', in B. Mitchell (ed.) *The Philosophy of Religion* (Oxford, 1971), and H. H. Price, *Belief* (London, 1969), Pt.II, Lecture 10.
11. See further P. Achinstein, *Law and Explanation* (Oxford, 1971), especially Chs VI–VII, for this kind of argument.
12. Geoffrey Parrinder, 'Religions of the East', in A. Toynbee (ed.) *Life After Death* (London, 1976), p.93.
13. Something of this idea survives in Kant's view of immortality as endless progress towards the complete accord of the will with the moral law (*Critique of Practical Reason*, II.ii.4).
14. See J. B. Lightfoot, *Notes on the Epistles of St. Paul* (London, 1895), pp.323–4.
15. I agree with Oscar Cullmann that art is the most suggestive medium here. See his remarks at the end of his 'Immortality of the Soul or Resurrection of the Dead', in K. Stendahl (ed.) *Immortality and Resurrection* (New York, 1965), p.53.
16. See Paul Badham, *Christian Beliefs about Life after Death* (London, 1976), Chs 4–5.
17. See Paul Helm, 'A Theory of Disembodied Survival and Re-embodied Existence', in *Religious Studies*, XIV (1978), 15–26.
18. See H. H. Price, 'Survival and the Idea of "Another World"', in J. R. Smythies (ed.) *Brain and Mind* (London, 1965); and *Essays in the Philosophy of Religion* (Oxford, 1972), pp.105–16.
19. See further M. Perry, *The Resurrection of Man* (London and Oxford, 1975), Ch. xi.
20. See M. de Unamuno, *The Tragic Sense of Life* (London, Fontana edn, 1967), especially Ch. x.
21. Hermann Cohen, *Religion of Reason out of the Sources of Judaism*, trans. S. Kaplan (New York, 1972), p.111. Much of his chapters on 'The Holy Spirit' (VII) and 'Immortality and Resurrection' (XV) is relevant to my argument.
22. St Paul envisages that gifts like prophecy and speaking in tongues will pass away, for they belong to an imperfect state (I Cor. xiii.8). Aquinas holds that the gifts of the Spirit mentioned in Isaiah xi.2 will remain in Heaven in their essence, though with a different operation (*S.T.* Ia.2ae.lxviii.6). Thus, for instance, fortitude will remain as confidence, rather than courage in the face of adversity; and counsel will still be needed to make the mind full of reason though not to prevent impetuosity (ibid., ad2).
23. A further consideration is introduced by John Morreall, who argues that belief in the resurrection of the body is superfluous if one believes in the Beatific Vision, for such a resurrection could add nothing to the perfect happiness to be enjoyed in the latter ('Perfect Happiness and the Resurrection of the Body', *Religious Studies*, XVI (1980), 29–35). But even if this is true, it fails to give any account of what is in question here, of how the Communion of Saints could be realised without a bodily resurrection.
24. Origen, *De Principiis*, III vi.4; *contra Celsum*, VII.32. See also *De Principiis*, II.xi.6

for his suggestion that the saints who die will remain in a place on this earth called Paradise for further instruction, after which they will ascend to a place in the air and reach the Kingdom of Heaven, passing through the spheres and globes (which scripture calls heavens). Such passages show that science-fiction-like descriptions of the future life are not a modern invention!

25. See C. F. D. Moule, 'St. Paul and Dualism: the Pauline Conception of Resurrection', in *New Testament Studies*, XII (1966), 108.

26. See R. J. Sider, 'The Pauline Conception of the Resurrection Body in I Cor. xv.35–54', *New Testament Studies*, XXI (1975), 428–39.

27. See also St Augustine, *The City of God*, XIII.20 for a similar interpretation.

CHAPTER 5:   Likeness to God

1. *De Principiis*, III.vi.1, trans. G. W. Butterworth, in Origen, *First Principles* (London, 1936), p.245.

2. *Adv. Haer.*, v.vi.1, trans. A. Roberts and W. H. Rambaut in *The Writings of Irenaeus* Vol. II (Edinburgh, 1869), p.68.

3. The *theological* distinction between 'image' and 'likeness' which both Origen and Irenaeus make is probably not licensed by the Hebrew of Gen. i.26, from which it derives. See David Cairns, *The Image of God in Man* (Fontana edn, London, 1973), p.28, and S. G. Wilson, 'Image of God', *Expository Times*, LXXXV (1974), 356–61.

4. See also Plato's *Republic* 500C, *Phaedrus* 248A, 252C–253C, *Laws* 717A.

5. Readers interested in pursuing it further may consult David Cairns, *Image of God in Man*; Vladimir Lossky, *In the Image and Likeness of God* (New York, 1974); G. Maloney, *Man the Divine Icon* (Pecos, New Mexico, 1973); John Passmore, *The Perfectibility of Man* (London, 1970); and E. J. Tinsley, *The Imitation of God in Christ* (London, 1960).

6. Among the more important texts are: Gen. i.26, v.1–3, ix.5f; Ps viii.6; Rom. viii.29; I Cor. xi.7, xv.49; II Cor. iii.18; Eph. iv.24, v.i; Phil. iii.21; Col. iii.10; I Jn iii.2; James iii.9; and in the Apocrypha: Wis. ii.23, Sir. xvii.3.

7. Matthew Arnold, *Literature and Dogma* (London, 1873), pp.306f. See F. von Hügel, *Essays and Addresses on the Philosophy of Religion*, II (London, 1926), pp.222f for a good discussion of God's likeness and unlikeness to His creation.

8. Though the Council of Chalcedon is content to say, paraphrasing Heb. iv.15 that in his manhood Christ was 'like us in all respects, apart from sin' (*Documents of the Christian Church*, Henry Bettenson (ed.) (Oxford, 1963), p.51.

9. Elsewhere I have suggested that such doublets have important implications for the scholastic doctrine of analogy. See my 'Analogy Today', *Philosophy* LI (1976), 431–46.

10. See D. S. Shapiro's excellent article 'The Doctrine of the Image of God and Imitatio Dei', in *Judaism*, XII (1963), 57–77. I owe much to conversations with Professor S. Schwarzschild on this topic.

11. See Moses Maimonides, *Guide to the Perplexed* I.54, III.54. They include mercy, graciousness and righteousness.

12. See his interesting discussion in *S.T.* Ia.2ae.lxi.5, where he defines four kinds of virtue: the social, perfecting, perfect, and exemplar virtues, the last of

which apply to God. Thus he says (ad 2) that the social virtues check the passions, the perfecting virtues uproot them, the perfect virtues (those of the Blessed in heaven and of man perfect in this life) forget them, and the exemplar virtues have no connection with them. This discussion can profit-ably be compared with his later discussion in la.2ae.lxviii.6, to which I have already alluded, about whether the gifts of the Holy Spirit remain in heaven. Aquinas concludes there (ad 2) that every gift includes something that passes away with the present state and something that remains in the future state. Thus fortitude will give us confidence, though there will no longer be that fortitude which fears not adversity; and counsel will still make our minds full of reason, though there will no longer be any need to prevent our being impetuous.

13. The relevant perfections are moral perfections. What, then, of God's other perfections, for instance His intelligence, knowledge and beauty? Are Albert Einstein and Marilyn Monroe more like Him than people of average intelli-gence and beauty? I think that we have to accept this conclusion, whilst noting that intelligence and beauty are only single attributes.

14. In contemporary English 'imitation' suggests an external relationship, copying or mimicking someone's actions. According to this usage, the 'imitation of Christ' might suggest a kind of legalism, in which the Gospel becomes a set of regulations, with the possibility of insincere and hypocriti-cal adhesion. But clearly, striving to become Christ-like is not an external copying, but involves a change in one's interior dispositions. In any case, there is no need to construe the word 'imitate' in a narrow sense, since the *Oxford English Dictionary* shows an older usage, according to which 'imitate' means 'become like'.

I suspect that Helmut Thielicke arbitrarily narrows the term in his discus-sion of the *imitatio Christi* in his *Theological Ethics*, Vol. I, trans W. H. Lazareth (London, 1968) Ch 10, especially pp.185f.

15. Besides the relationship of transitivity there is also that of *symmetry* to be considered. Likeness, as Plato pointed out (*Parmenides* 132D), is a symmetrical relationship: if I am like you, then you are like me. On the other hand, the relationship of 'being [in] the image of' is not symmetrical: Aquinas rightly notes that the notion of an 'image' adds something to that of 'likeness', for it suggests the idea of an imprint taken from another, or an imitation; thus one egg is like another, but is not its image (*S.T.* la.xciii.1). Because 'image' suggests a priority (often a causal priority, for example a reflection in water or in a mirror, caused by an object), it is not a symmetrical relationship (though the likeness involved is symmetrical).

It is, of course, necessary to specify in virtue of what a likeness holds: it would not be very illuminating to be told 'My love is like a lettuce'. More-over, each attribute may have a quantitative variation (for instance, degrees of intensity of colour). Thus total resemblance would require both exact resemblance with regard to each single characteristic and complete resemblance in the list of characteristics involved (see H. H. Price, *Thinking and Experience*, London, 1953, Ch. 1). Still, from a logical point of view, it follows that if a man is like God in some respect, then God is like that man. But theologians have sought to introduce qualifications here: indeed, Aquinas denies that the symmetry holds (*S.T.* la.iv.3 ad 4), and is taken to task by John Passmore for confusing the relationships of likeness, which is symmetrical, and 'is a likeness of', which is not so (*The Perfectibility of Man*, London, 1970, p.71).

This criticism is warranted, but of course Aquinas has *theological* reasons for rejecting the symmetry: he holds that God is outside any *genus*, so there can be only an analogical likeness between Him and creatures (*S.T.* Ia.iv.3, ad 3); moreover God's perfections pre-exist in Him unitedly and simply – indeed, He *is* goodness, love and so on, in which creatures participate (*S.T.* Ia.iii.3, ad 1; vi.4; xiii.4; *Expos. de Hebdomadibus* 5), so that for Aquinas any talk of God being like creatures might involve a regressive Third Man argument. Duns Scotus allows for common concepts between God and creatures in virtue of their likeness, but says they are not 'generically common' (*Op.Ox.* I.viii.3.10ff).

16. St Cyril of Alexandria, *Capita Argumentorum* of his *Dialogue on the Holy Spirit* (*P.G.* lxxv: 1144).
17. St Cyril of Alexandria, *Thesaurus on the Holy and Undivided Trinity* 34 (*P.G.* lxxv: 597). See also Athanasius, *ad Serap.* I.24 and Basil, *On the Holy Spirit*, §23.
18. For instance by St Gregory Nazianzen (*Orations* xxxi.28–30; xli.9–12).
19. Basil, *On the Holy Spirit*, §§23, 38.
20. William of St Thierry, *The Golden Epistle*, trans. J. McCann and W. Shewring (London, 1930), Ch. 16, §§62, 68; also in *The Works of William of St. Thierry*, Vol. 4, trans. J. Berkeley (Kalamazoo, 1976), pp.94–6, 102–3.

    St John of the Cross speaks of the 'union of likeness', which exists when God's will and ours are in conformity: cf. his *The Ascent of Mount Carmel*, II.v.3–4, and *The Spiritual Canticle* (2nd Redaction), xxxviii.3.
21. For example in Acts xvi.7. See James Dunn, *Jesus and the Spirit* (London, 1975), §54, for relevant references and a discussion of them.
22. *Ad Serap.* I.20, 24, 26; iv.3. See the discussion of these passages in G. Maloney, *Man the Divine Icon* (Pecos, New Mexico, 1973), Ch. 6.
23. St John of Damascus, *Exposition on the Orthodox Faith*, Bk.I, Ch. 13. Aquinas says that the Holy Spirit is like *both* the Father and the Son, though only the Son is the image of the Father (*S.T.* Ia.xxxv.2).
24. E. J. Tinsley, *The Imitation of God in Christ* (London, 1960), p.165. Compare the discussion of this question by James Dunn, *Jesus and the Spirit*, who goes on to remark that the origins of the doctrine of the Trinity are in human experience (p.326). I think that this is true; but of course we have to go a long way to show how people come to conclude that the Holy Spirit is a distinct person or *hypostasis* within the undivided Trinity, and to justify this conclusion.
25. Likewise, St Gregory of Nyssa often appeals to the concept of *epektasis*, the constant stretching out of the soul towards perfection, for example in *Sermon* 8: 'The graces that we receive at every point are indeed great, but the path that lies beyond our immediate grasp is infinite ... those who thus share in the divine Goodness ... will always enjoy a greater and greater participation in grace throughout all eternity' (*P.G.* xliv.940–1, trans. H. Musurillo).
26. Quoted by R. T. Herbert, *Paradox and Identity in Theology* (Ithaca, N.Y., 1979), p.174.
27. Norman Malcolm, *Ludwig Wittgenstein: a Memoir* (London, 1966), p.71. This

suggestion may be contrasted with his remark in the *Tractatus* that the supposition of a life after death would solve nothing (6.4312).

28. Immanuel Kant, *Critique of Practical Reason*, Bk.II, Ch. 2, §§4, 6, 7.
29. Cf. D. Z. Phillips, *Religion without Explanation* (Oxford, 1976), Ch. 6.
30. As perhaps W. E. Channing's cruder treatment suggests. See his sermon 'Likeness to God', in Vol. III of his *Works* (Boston, Mass., 1843).
31. A fuller discussion of Aquinas' argument on these points would require a consideration of his teaching on analogy, of which they are part. Again, see my article 'Analogy Today', already cited in note 9 above. There I also discuss Duns Scotus' views: he too adopts the procedure of the *via remotionis* and the *via eminentiae*, although disagreeing with some of Aquinas' teaching on analogy.
32. F. von Hügel, *Eternal Life* (2nd edn, Edinburgh, 1913), p.238.

CHAPTER 6: Conclusion

1. See my *Religion, Truth and Language-Games* (London, 1977), p.136.
2. See Bernard Williams, *Problems of the Self* (Cambridge, 1973), pp.8–11.
3. For such arguments see John Hick, *Death and Eternal Life* (London, 1976), Ch. 15; Bruce R. Reichenbach, 'Recreationism and Personal Identity', *Christian Scholars Review*, IV (1975), 326–30, 'Monism and the Possibility of Life After Death', *Religious Studies*, XIV (1978), 27–34; and Robert Young, 'The Resurrection of the Body', *Sophia*, IX (1970), 1–15, 'Professor Penelhum on the Resurrection of the Body', *Religious Studies*, IX (1973), 181–7.
4. Paul Helm, 'A Theory of Disembodied Survival and Re-embodied Existence', *Religious Studies*, XIV (1978) 15–26. Of course, many of Helm's arguments could be used merely to defend the idea of disembodied survival, rather than the 'two-stage' view. Richard Purtill uses similar arguments in his 'The Intelligibility of Disembodied Survival', *Christian Scholars Review*, V (1975), 3–22: for instance, against Penelhum he argues that a soul might remember having done something in its bodily stage, even though it now lacks a body, and that if there were other observers of the action, then the memory claim *is* checkable.
5. Bernard Williams, *Problems of the Self*, Ch. 6. Richard Swinburne remarks tartly that those whom Williams envisages as being bored in the after-life seem to be persons of limited idealism (*Faith and Reason*, Oxford, 1981, p.135). Compare Swift's Struldbruggs, who live on in an earthly setting without dying, and become peevish and melancholy (*Gulliver's Travels*, Pt. III, Ch. 10).
6. St John of the Cross, *The Spiritual Canticle* (2nd Redaction), xii.8; xxxix.1, 4, 6, 10; *The Living Flame of Love* (2nd Redaction), i.6; ii.21, 34; ii, 78.
7. See John Clarke, 'Mysticism and the Paradox of Survival', *International Philosophical Quarterly*, VI (1971), 165–79, and Louis Bouyer, *Le Consolateur: Esprit Saint et vie de Grâce* (Paris, 1980), p.420.
8. See Joseph P. Gibbons, 'Brightman's Philosophy of Immortality', *The Personalist*, LIV (1973), 176–87, and A. E. Taylor, 'The Belief in Immortality', in F. J. Foakes-Jackson, *Faith and the War* (London, 1915). Such a view has to face the question of whether we can be tempted in the future life.

John Hick in his *Death and Eternal Life* (London, 1976) sees the continuous purification as occurring through a series of reincarnations in 'other spaces', thus combining, it would seem, the Catholic doctrine of Purgatory with a version of belief in reincarnation. In his interesting and perceptive review of the book Terence Penelhum makes the point that, in the absence of memories reaching back into previous lives, similarity of disposition and other very weak sources of individuation are all that remain to give content to the idea of individual continuance. But since identity goes closely with memory, 'the argument for a multiplicity of future lives, rather than the long one with sub-phases, loses its force' (*Canadian Journal of Philosophy*, IX (1979), 160). Hick has already himself criticised Eastern doctrines of reincarnation earlier in the book and it is doubtful whether his own version of it is necessary to give content to the notion of gradually reaching perfection.

9. Michael Perry argues along these lines in *The Resurrection of Man* (London and Oxford, 1975), Chs XI–XII . But H. H. Price suggests that social life in the next world might take place through 'telepathic apparitions' (in J. R. Smythies, *Brain and Mind*, London, 1965, pp.10f).

10. H. Wheeler Robinson, 'Personality and the Life Beyond', in James Marchant (ed.), *Life after Death* (London, 1925), p.52.

11. Abbé Huvelin, *Some Spiritual Guides of the Seventeenth Century* (New York, 1927), p.lxxvi. The Abbé Huvelin (1838–1910) was a Parisian priest, who deeply influenced men as diverse as Blondel, Charles de Foucauld, von Hügel and Emile Littré by his spiritual counsels. See M.-T.-L. Lefebvre, *Abbé Huvelin, Apostle of Paris* (Dublin, 1967).

12. Since the argument turns on falsification rather than verification, it may be applicable to other religions besides Christianity. And, as I explained in Chapter 3, the existence of non-Christian saints is not a difficulty for Christians, unless they claim that the Holy Spirit is given *only* to Christians. The statement in the creed that the Holy Spirit spoke through the prophets indicates that the early church recognised the presence of the Spirit in pre-Christian times (as my quotation from St Leo on p.49 also indicates), although it regarded such a presence as a mere glimmer of what was to come at Pentecost and afterwards.

13. See Peter Brown, *The Cult of the Saints* (London, 1981) for a fascinating account of the beginnings of some of those practices and beliefs.

14. Michael Perham, *The Communion of Saints* (London, 1980), p.48. See also Barth's discussion of the Sanctification of Man, in *C.D.* I V.ii, §66.

15. The position of the Anglican Church is more complex: for a good treatment see Perham, *Communion of Saints*, especially Chs 5–6.

Index